THE ROAD TO CROSSBARRY

The Decisive Battle of Ireland's War of Independence 1919-21

Diarmuid Begley

D1615047

2nd Edition 2002

Published by
DESO PUBLICATIONS
1 Meadowlands,
Courtmacsherry,
Co. Cork,
Ireland.
Telephone: 00 353 23 46683
Email: dbegley@tinet.ie

ISBN 0 9536099 0 1

Cover photograph courtesy of The Examiner.

Printed by Litho Press Co., Midleton, Co. Cork, Ireland.

What can ye know of spirits such as these
or of the powers that move them to great deeds
'gainst frightful odds ?.
What did they do? you say who will not see,
Nor judge their merits further than their gains,
They gave their lives — no more!.

Grace Lorenza O'Malley

Today more than ever there is a great need to return to the national ideals, to re-instate all that is good but conveniently pushed aside by greed, materialism, revisionism and other evils.

ACKNOWLEDGEMENTS

I wish to express my sincere gratitude to the following who in their diverse ways helped me in the preparation of this tribute to every man and woman who played a part, no matter how small, in Ireland's War of Independence 1919-1921.

Brian Kearney, Dublin.

Paddy Connolly, T.C. Bandon. Co. Cork.

Mrs. Mary O'Sullivan (nee Lordan), Mallow. Co. Cork.

Liam Healy, Cork City.

Jim Barrett, Dunmanway Road, Bandon, Co. Cork.

John Lordan, Coolanagh. Newcwstown. Co. Cork.

Mrs. Mary Twomey, Timoleague. Co. Cork.

Mrs. Elenor O'Sullivan (nee O'Connell), Eyeries. Co Cork.

Sean Hales, Knocknacurra. Co.Cork.

Mrs. Mary Kiely, Beal na Blath, Crookstown. Co. Cork.

Sean Kelleher, Bandon, Co. Cork.

Mrs. Margaret Shorten (nee Callanan), Bandon. Co. Cork.

Michael Lyons, Bandon. Co. Cork.

My thanks to Anita Begley (Dublin), Nuala O'Farrell (Birmingham), Sean Ward (Cork), Brian Kearney, (Dublin), and Paddy Connolly, (Bandon), for reading and correcting some of the many drafts of the manuscript over the last three years.

To my wife Elsie and my family for their patience and tolerence throughout.

A special word of thanks to my daughter Orlaith and her husband Denis for putting up with me for weeks on end in their home in Goleen and to Orlaith for putting the first draft on computor for me and really getting me started.

PHOTOGRAPHS

I wish to express my gratitude for the use of photographs to the following:

Donal Sheehan, Photographer, Cork.

Michael Lyons, Bandon.

Paddy Connolly, Bandon.

Dan Joe O'Mahony, Bandon.

John Lordan, Coolanagh, Newcestown.

Mrs. Margaret Shorten, Bandon.

The Examiner, Cork.

FOREWORD

I first attended school in 1949 at St. Fintan's National School, Bandon. At that time, Ireland, through the efforts and sacrifices of the previous generation of men and women, was free and independent, had its own government and its own Department of Education for almost 20 years. Yet, I can honestly say, that the Department of Education then, and up to the mid to late fifties, when I left secondary education, seemed either ashamed or unable to sanction any school history book which dealt with the men and women of 1919 to 1921 and their final victory over the forces of the Crown.

There were of course many teachers whose outlook was nationalistic and it was because of their pride in our independence, that my generation was first introduced to the Easter rising of 1916 and to the War of Independence, but even then there were very meagre chapters, if any, in the school history books now produced and published by Irish firms and sanctioned by the Department of Education. By 1950 Grants History of Europe was on our history course at secondary school and it dealt with England's victory over Germany and Japan in the Second World War of 1939 to 1945 but to my knowledge we still did not have a history book which dealt with our War of Independence of 1919 to 1921.

In the late forties I first read "Rebel Corks Fighting Story" published by the "Kerryman" newspaper in 1947.

Then on to "Limericks Fighting Story" and "Dublin's Fighting Story" and any article or book that dealt with that significant chapter of Irish History that I could lay my hands on. I read of the men and women who fought, suffered and in many cases died so that Ireland could take its place among the Nations of the World with pride and realised that many of them were men and women coming into my fathers shop week after week I saw them in a whole new light, how proud I was of these quiet unassuming men and women who had left their homes and families to take on the best trained, battle hardened soldiers in the world and won!. I knew those wonderful men and women and I often spoke to them in our shop, but as yet, in 1950, I would not dare to question them of their contribution to our Independence. All of that was to change in a couple of years.

By 1952 I was no longer a "boy", I could ask questions about the "trouble" times of my parents and their contemporaries and though some of the answers were a little guarded, I learned more and more of what it meant to live in Ireland, prior to, and during the War of Independence and the pride of being Irish and free grew in me. The answers to some of my questions were a long time coming because the questions would have been deemed sensitive, but, those answers came too, with the passage of time.

I read of the fight for freedom up and down the country ; of Dan Breen, Sean Tracey, the Kents, Austin Stack, Liam Deasy, Tom Barry and Liam Lynch; of the Brigade Officers, the Battalion Officers, the Company Captains, the Lieutenants, the active service men, the scouts, the keymen at the river crossings, the young boys and the postal and railway employees, who contributed so much and of the women who carried so much of the load, most of the grief, and without whom there could not have been a War of Independence.

I could not read and learn enough about the time that was in it. Thank God most of what I have read was written prior to the arrival of the revisionists on the scene, with their apologetic accounts, so much at variance with what I had heard from participants. (They are really the "spur" that made me agree to write this appreciation of the gallant men of the Battle of Crossbarry, the members of the Third (West) Cork Brigade, and the wives and sisters who supported them.)

I want my children, my grandchildren and their generations to read of Crossbarry as it happened. To pass on to them a pride in the men and women, their grandparents and great grandparents, who gained for my generation, this generation and generations to come, the right to live and work in our country, independent and free. I want them to read of what really happened before the revisionists come up with their further apologies for our history and for those men and women who made it happen.

To do this, it is very necessary to fill in the background to the War of Independence and to introduce the reader to the way things were in Ireland prior to July 11th 1921 when the mighty British Empire called for a truce.

To deal properly with the Battle of Crossbarry, the final great chapter of the War of Independence, it is necessary first, to give the young readers a brief synopsis of the events which brought this about. In doing so, I will deal very briefly with the main events of the period from 1858 to 1916 in chronological order and hope that my efforts will stimulate a desire in them for more detailed knowledge of that period of our history. At the end of this story I will list some of the sources where the quest for further knowledge will be satisfied

TABLE OF CONTENTS

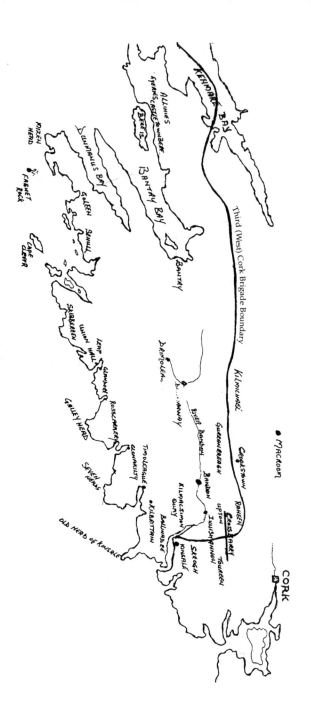

The West Cork Brigade Area

KENMARE BAY

ALLIHIES
'FERNS CASTLE' DUNBEAR
BERE IS.
BANTRY BAY

POZEN HEAD
FASNET ROCK

DUNMANUS BAY

GOLEEN

SCHULL

CAPE CLEAR

BANTRY

Third (West) Cork Brigade Boundary

SKIBBEREEN

UNION HALL

GLANDORE

DRINDLEAH

ROSSCARBERY

GALLEY HEAD

TIMOLEAGUE
CLONAKILTY

SEVEN HEADS

KILBRITTAIN

OLD HEAD OF KINSALE

BALLINADEE

KILMACSIMON QUAY

KINSALE

SKEOGH

TOUREEN
INNISHANNON
UPTON

KILMICHAEL

CROOKSTOWN

River Bandon

SHANNONVALE

BANDON

CROSS BARRY

GUENOUREAGH

BANDON

MACROOM

CORK

THE BEGINNING

In the years 1798, 1803, 1848 and in 1867 Irishmen took up arms in order to break with England. Each rebellion was crushed mercilessly, with the leaders and their supporters executed or transported to the furthest corners of the British Empire.

1858

In 1858 the majority of the people of Ireland lived in abject poverty under the landlord class, and if they were unable to meet the high rents demanded, then they were evicted from their dwellings. These rents were constantly being increased, in many cases to bring about the eviction of the poor wretches so that their hovel could be levelled, thus enabling the landlord to escape the Government tax now levied on every building on his property.

James Stephens

As the number of evictions increased, so also did the resentment of the people towards the landlords (many of whom lived in Britain), their agents, most of whom were Irish and in many cases were merciless towards their less fortunate fellow Irishmen, and towards the British Government. Once again in Irish history a movement dedicated to total separation from Britain was founded. It was to be known as the Irish Republican Brotherhood (I.R.B.) and it's leader was James Stephens. The Irish Republican Brotherhood was also established in the United States and a fellow republican, who had escaped to America after the 1848 rebellion and who was now the leader of the organisation there, suggested that the members of the I.R.B. should now be known as "Fenians". This recommendation was accepted by all members on both sides of the Atlantic. Fenianism grew among the Irish in America, in Britain, and at home.

1865

In the years following 1858, the Fenians drilled and practised the use of firearms in the hills throughout Ireland. Fenianism was alsovery strong among the urban artisan classes. The Irish people however, were indifferent if not hostile, to the movement. Now, in 1865, Stephens, along with three other leaders of the Fenians, John O'Leary, Thomas Clarke Luby, and Jeremiah O'Donovan-Rossa (Skibbereen), were arrested. They were brought for trial to Green St, Court in Dublin where they were convicted and sentenced. O'Leary and Luby were each given 20 years penal servitude. O'Donovan-Rossa was sentenced to penal servitude for life. James Stephens escaped dramatically on the eve of his trial and made his way to America.

John O'Leary

1867

With the founder now in America and with many of its leaders in prison, the Fenian movement was disorganised and suffered from the lack of good leadership. However, it was decided to raise a rebellion but, though many thousands of the Fenians turned out, due to lack of arms; lack of leadership; lack of co-ordination and despite their heroism, it failed miserably. Hundreds were arrested, tried and sentenced.

Before being sent to the convict prisons in England and the Colonies, most of the Fenian prisoners were incarcerated in Mountjoy Prison in Dublin. This prison was built by convict labour during the Famine period and from the beginning it had an ignominious history. In 1866 there were 226 suspects in Mountjoy and in 1867, seven prisoners, all untried, were driven insane.

In the English convict prisons, Millbank, Pentonville, Woking, Chatham and Dartmoor, the treatment of the Fenian prisoners was much worse. O'Leary, Kickham, and Luby were required to hew rocks, carry flagstones, serve bricks and dig trenches, while O'Donovan-Rossa, manacled hand and foot, had to eat his food from a bowl on the floor like a dog.

An American Fenian, Dr. Thomas Gallagher, who had left America on March 14th 1883, was arrested ten days after his arrival in England. He was charged with complicity to blow up buildings with dynamite and sentenced to life impisonment. Through the intervention of the United States Government he and another prisoner named Whitehead, were released, insane,on August 25th 1896. Dr. Anthony Mac Bride, a brother of Major John Mac Bride, had to escort him to New York. Another American, Sgt. Mac Carthy, on the morning of his release with Michael Davitt, dropped dead from his treament in prison as they were about to meet Parnell in a Dublin hotel.

1870

In this year a Home Government Association for Ireland was founded by Isaac Butt, "Father of Home Rule" a Dublin Protestant lawyer, and leader of the Irish Parliamentary Party at Westminster. The aim of this association was to obtain an Irish Parliament to legislate for Irish affairs and it was hoped that the Irish Members of Parliament would press for Home Rule.

Isaac Butt

1875

Charles Stewert Parnell, a Protestant landlord, was elected Member of Parliament at Westminster for Meath in 1875. Although he was an advocate of Home Rule for Ireland, he had little in common with his fellow Irish members there. However, he developed the strategy of "obstruction through debate" in Parliament to focus attention on Irish issues. He was extremely successful in this and while he became a constant nuisance to the British, he became more and more popular back home in Ireland.

1880

In this year, Parnell took over the leadership of the Irish Parliamentary Party from Isaac Butt.

Next he became President of the Irish Land League which had been founded by Michael Davitt in 1879 to procure better conditions for the tenant farmers of Ireland. He advocated the boycott of unreasonable landlords and their agents to the members of the Land League. As a result of the agitation of the League the then Prime Minister, William Gladstone, introduced a Coercion Act in Parliament which provided for the imprisonment without trial of anyone suspected of lawlessness.

1881

Although the Coercion Act became law, Parnell and Davitt exhorted the members of the Land League to defy the law and they were both, along with many others, arrested and imprisoned. Now Parnell became more popular then ever and, on his release from prison in 1882, he was regarded by most as the leader of the Irish people, the "Uncrowned King of Ireland".

1884

The Gaelic Athletic Association was founded in Hayes' Hotel in Thurles for the promotion of our national games and culture.

Charles Stewart Parnell

1885

At this time the Irish Parliamentary Party (I.P.P.) held the balance of power at Westminster and they forced Gladstone, the Liberal Prime Minister, to introduce a Bill for Home Rule for Ireland in 1886. This Bill was defeated in the House of Commons on June 8th 1886 by 343 votes to 313. Gladstone believed that some sort of Home Rule for Ireland would bring peace to the country. The Ulster Unionists (Orangemen) on the other hand had threatened armed resistance against the Bill if passed.

Shortly after the defeat of the Bill, Parnell was cited as co-respondent in a divorce case. He did not defend or deny it and under pressure from Gladstone, the majority of the Irish Parliamentary Party forced Parnell to step down from the leadership of the party.

1890

Now the Party split. The majority, led by Justin Mc Carthy, rejected Parnell while the minority, led by John Redmond, remained loyal to him.

1891

Parnell, now in bad health, died in England in October 1891, aged 45 years.

1892

In 1892 Gladstone again introduced another Home Rule for Ireland Bill in Parliament. There was vigorous opposition to the Bill throughout Ireland and in Parliament but nowhere was this opposition so great as in Ulster.

Here the Unionists saw the Bill as the end of their very existence. To be ruled in future from Dublin by an Irish Parliament? No, Never!!!

They were supported by the Conservative Party (who espoused the Unionist cause in Parliament) and by the Southern Unionists in Ireland. Lord Randolph Churchill (father of Winston) was sent over to Belfast to guarantee the support of the Conservatives.

1893

The Home Rule Bill was passed in the House of Commons. The Irish Parliamentary Party were jubilant, as were Gladstone and his Liberal Party. The Bill now went before the House of Lords where, on September 8th. 1893, it was defeated by 419 votes to 41.

After this defeat, the Liberal Party determined to curb the powers of the House of Lords so that the Lords could never again reject a Bill that had passed through all stages in the House of Commons. In 1895 they were ousted from power before they could achieve this aim.

During the visit of Sir Randolph Churchill (father of Winston) to Ulster to guarantee the support of the Conservative Party in Britain to the Unionist opposition to the Home Rule Bill, he exhorted them to play the "Orange Card". It was as a result of this endorsement of what was hitherto looked upon as a disreputable organisation that the Loyal Orange Order became a seemingly respectable organisation.

In 1892 they had threatened to oppose Home Rule for Ireland by all means, force of arms if necessary, against the British Parliament!

After the defeat of Gladstone's second Home Rule Bill the Unionists of Ulster endeavoured to enrol every loyalist, of every class, into one organisation.

THE GUN INTRODUCED INTO IRISH POLITICS

1893

In this year, the Gaelic League was founded by Dr.Douglas Hyde, the son of the Rector of the Church of Ireland in Tibohone, Frenchpark, Co. Roscommon. His love of the Irish Language came from listening to folklore from the old people around his childhood home. Within a few years the Gaelic League had over 500 branches throughout Ireland teaching written and oral Irish, Irish music and dancing.

Dr. Douglas Hyde was to have a profound influence on all aspects of Irish Culture for all of his life. He was a co-founder of the Abbey Theatre. He wrote the first play in Irish to be performed professionally, "Casadh an tSugain" and wrote a number of other popular plays. He became the first President of Ireland in 1938.

1896

James Connolly formed the Irish Republican Socialist Party to further the cause of the Irish workers for better conditions.

After 1898, the centenary of rebellion of the United Irishmen, patriotism grew strong once again, Arthur Griffith founded a newspaper "The United Irishman". . The Gaelic League, fostering the revival of the Irish language, spread throughout the country. The Irish Republican Brotherhood, formed by James Stephens in 1858 for the overthrow by force of British rule in Ireland, gained many recruits from the Gaelic League and Sinn Fein, but by 1905, numbers in that organisation had fallen away again as nationalistic fervour waned.

1899

Arthur Griffith was Editor of the "United Irishman" newspaper in which he wrote: "Lest there be a doubt in any mind, we will say that we accept the Nationalism of '48, '67, and '98 (three unsuccessful uprisings against British rule) as the true Nationalism, and Grattan's cry, "Live Ireland--perish the Empire!" as the watchword of patriotism." (United Irishman March 4th. 1899).

Arthur Griffith

In 1904 a friend of his, Mary Butler, suggested that he change the name of his newspaper ("United Irishman") to "Sinn Fein" and in 1905 he founded the Sinn Fein movement, an organisation which sought political salvation through passive means and advocated economic nationalism.

1900

John Redmond became leader of the Irish Parliamentary Party and again pushed for Home Rule for Ireland but only by peaceful means.

John Redmond

A form of Home Rule for Ireland had been suggested for some years past and in the first years of the 20th century, at any suggestion of unrest in the country, it was trotted out again as being just around the corner. By 1910 the Liberals had come to power in Britain and many felt that now, at last, Home Rule for Ireland would be granted. However any suggestion of Home Rule for Ireland was bitterly opposed by Unionists throughout Ireland, not only the decendants of Planters but also a Catholic middle class which enjoyed economic advantage

Agitation, first on constitutional lines and later on treasonable lines, manifested itself among the decendants of the Scottish-English borderers who had been the original Planters in Ulster.

1910

The Unionists first threatened armed resistance to Home Rule in 1892 and introduced the gun to Irish Political life for the first time. The second indication of armed resistence to the Home Rule proposal appears in the manifests of the Grand Orange Lodge of Ireland in December 1910 "You must use every effort to defeat them (the Redmondites) at the polls, neglecting no opportunity of influencing votes in Great Britain, but you are equally bound to prepare for a struggle in this country if we fail to carry the elections. Already steps are being taken to enrol men to meet any emergency".

1911

On September 23rd 1911, according to police estimates 300,000 people congregated at the home of Captain Craig (later to become the first Prime Minister of Northern Ireland). The principal speaker at this gathering was Sir Edward Carson. He re-affirmed that the Ulster Unionist Council (founded in 1904)would never accept Home Rule. He hinted at plans to set up a provisional government for Ulster, using force if necessary.

1912

The third Home Rule for Ireland bill was introduced in the House of Commons by Mr.Asquith, the Liberal Prime Minister, on April 11th 1912. John Redmond, of the Irish Parliamentary Party, accepted it as the final solution for Ireland and exhorted Irishmen everywhere to refrain from force of arms as Home Rule was now attainable by peaceful means.However, the Irish Republican Brotherhood, Sinn Fein, and the other Nationalist groups held no brief for Redmond or his Home Rule Bill as they would only settle for complete and total seperation from England.

1912

On Saturday, September 28th, "Ulster Day", a solemn pledge, protesting their loyalty to the King but also to use all means which were thought necessary to defeat the Home Rule Bill, was taken by those who signed the Solemn League and Covenant. It was estimated that over 200,000 men signed this pledge.

Sir Edward Carson

At this point, the English Unionists (the Conservatives) led by Bonar Law, aligned themselves with the Ulster Unionists to defeat the Bill. Lord Carson stated, "We must be prepared, the morning Home Rule passes, ourselves to to become responsible for the government of the Protestant Province of Ulster".

In December 1912 a decision was taken to enrol an Ulster Volunteer Force (U.V.F.) for military service in the campaign against Home Rule for Ireland. This force came into being in January 1913.

Ulster's
Solemn League and Covenant.

Being convinced in our consciences that Home Rule would be disastrous to the material well-being of Ulster as well as of the whole of Ireland, subversive of our civil and religious freedom, destructive of our citizenship and perilous to the unity of the Empire, we, whose names are underwritten, men of Ulster, loyal subjects of His Gracious Majesty King George V., humbly relying on the God whom our fathers in days of stress and trial confidently trusted, do hereby pledge ourselves in solemn Covenant throughout this our time of threatened calamity to stand by one another in defending for ourselves and our children our cherished position of equal citizenship in the United Kingdom and in using all means which may be found necessary to defeat the present conspiracy to set up a Home Rule Parliament in Ireland. ¶ And in the event of such a Parliament being forced upon us we further solemnly and mutually pledge ourselves to refuse to recognise its authority. ¶ In sure confidence that God will defend the right we hereto subscribe our names. ¶ And further, we individually declare that we have not already signed this Covenant.

The above was signed by me at _____
"Ulster Day," Saturday, 28th September, 1912.

—— God Save the King. ——

The Ulster Covenant

1913

Now the Ulster Unionists set up the Ulster Provisional Government.

By September 1913 the Ulster Volunteer Force numbered 56,000 men and was commanded by Major General Sir George Richardson K.C.B.. Parades were held throughout the North of Ireland with speeches being delivered by Sir Edward Carson who could claim no connection, historic, family or otherwise with Ulster having been born in Dublin. The legality of these Ulster Volunteer Force meetings and parades was, on referral to the Law Offices of the Crown, found to be felonius. Many thought that this challenge to British Authority and to Westminster would be suppressed by the Government but this was not to be. The Government did not take any action against the Unionists and so they became more daring, more traitorous and more dangerous. They landed arms at Larne, Bangor and Donaghadee. These arms were procured in Germany and the man detailed to purchase them was Fred Crawford, an old Militia officer. He was a fanatic who was said to have signed the Ulster Covenant with his own blood.

1914

The Government ordered the British Army, stationed in the Curragh, Co. Kildare, to march North in a show of strength, but many of the Officers resigned their commissions rather than march against the Unionists. This bordered on mutiny and the incident, in fact, became known as the "Curragh Mutiny". The British Government took no action against these officers and all were re-instated to former ranks.

Thus, in May 1914, the Unionists were able to dictate to the British Government, their Government, to amend the Government of Ireland Bill. The final reading of that Bill was passed on the undertaking that an amending Bill, to exclude parts of Ulster from the provisions of the original Bill, would be introduced. So much for Home Rule for Ireland!

The arms landed at Larne, Bangor and Donaghadee were distributed all over Ulster and the British Government was now faced with the rebel army of the Ulster Unionist Council.

FORMATION OF THE IRISH VOLUNTEERS

Though the numbers of the Irish Republican Brotherhood had fallen away by 1905, the organisation was nonetheless alive and well with recruitment continuing throughout the country. At this time there were three parties representing Ireland in the British parliament.

(a) The Irish Parliamentary Party led by John Redmond.

(b) The Ulster Unionist Party led by Sir Edward Carson.

(c) The "All for Ireland League" led by William O'Brien.

The Irish Parliamentary Party (or Redmondites) were strongest in the South, though the "All for Ireland League" (or O'Brienites) were very strong in Cork.

The Ulster Unionist Party held sway in the north east of Ulster.

1913

In 1913 the leaders of the Irish Republican Brotherhood, on seeing that the Unionists had landed arms unopposed at Larne and Bangor, argued that they too could seize the opportunity to create a open military organisation in the South. Eoin McNeill, Con Colbert, Tom Clarke, Sean McDermott and others decided that if the Orangemen of Ulster could arm themselves against England so could the Irish Republican Brotherhood come into the open against England.

On November 25th 1913 a huge meeting was held in the Rotunda Rink in Dublin and a new volunteer army was launched, the Irish Volunteers. Soon branches were being formed all over the country. Con Colbert was on the Provisional Committee of the Irish Volunteers and, in selecting and training officers, he aimed at creating a nucleus of Irish Republican Brotherhood Officers. Later when John Redmond forced his way on to the Provisional Executive Committee of the Irish Volunteers with the intention of controlling it, he was opposed by Colbert, Pearse, Mallin, Ceannt, Mellows and Mac Diarmada. All six of these men were later to die in Kilmainham Jail for their part in the 1916 Rising.

On December 16th 1913 the Constitution of the Irish Volunteers was ratified. The objects were:

1. To secure and maintain the rights and liberties common to all the people of Ireland.
2. To train, discipline, arm and equip a body of Irish Volunteers for the above purpose.
3. To unite for this purpose Irishmen of every creed and of every party and class.

11

On July 25th 1914 at Howth in Co. Dublin, 900 German rifles were landed in an effort to arm the new Volunteer Army. On August 5th another consignment of arms was landed at Kilcool, Co. Wicklow. In contrast to their lack of action against the Orangemen at Larne and Bangor, the British now tried, without success, to disarm the volunteers as they marched from Howth into Dublin. The Kings Own Scottish Borderers fired into an unarmed crowd at Batcholar's Walk.

Molly Childers on the Asgard

At the outbreak of the First World War in this year John Redmond exhorted the Irish Volunteers to support England in the war against Germany and that, in return, Ireland would possibly get Home Rule at last. He openly recruited for the British army throughout the country and even pledged the support of the Irish Volunteers to the British war effort. This action split the Irish Volunteers into two camps.

1. The Redmondites or National Volunteers.
2. Oglaigh na hEireann or the Irish Volunteers.

Remembering the past expectations of Ireland from the British Parliament and their failure to materialise, the leaders of the Irish Volunteers could see no value in Redmond's idea and were now in direct conflict with John Redmond and the National Volunteers. This conflict of views resulted in many branches of the New Volunteer Army, which had sprung up after the historic meeting at the Rotunda Rink in 1913, splitting into camps or disbanding altogether.

1914

In this same year at the Buckingham Palace Conference on the fate of Ulster, the Home Rule Act was suspended (and again in 1915 and 1916), until one year after the end of the war. John Redmond and his supporters agreed to this.

1915

In 1915 the recruiting campaign for the British army was in full swing throughout Ireland with meetings being held all over the country to entice young Irishmen to go to the aid of "Little Catholic Belgium" against the Germans. Some recruiting posters depicted a Church in flames in an effort to persuade young men to enlist. There were not any posters or information available to explain to those men that "Poor Catholic Belgium" was one of the largest Colonial powers in Africa and was treating the people of it's colonies in the same fashion as the British had been treating the Irish for seven hundred years. To counter this the Irish Volunteers queried the subjection, by the British, of "Poor Catholic Ireland". They disrupted these meetings and tore down the recruiting posters as fast as they were put up.

Recruits for the British Army came mainly from the towns, primarily from the lack of opportunities for employment, and partially from a desire for adventure, although the poor recruits could have had no knowledge of the horror awaiting them on the Western Front.

The Sinn Fein movement was strongest in rural areas.

In 1915 the majority of the people of Ireland supported John Redmond and his Parliamentary Party and very few recruits for the Irish Volunteers were to be found.

In the autumn of 1915 the war was not going well for Britain and the casualties in her army were huge. It was felt in Ireland that conscription might be introduced and, while such a development had not yet materialised, an increase in the number of young men joining the ranks of Sinn Fein became evident. Yet the Volunteers and their supporters still formed a very very small percentage of the population, only 3%.

1916

Then came the Rising of Easter 1916 in Dublin and the savage executions of the leaders. If the British Government had not executed the 1916 leaders in Kilmainham Jail with such indecent haste it might have been many years before the people would have supported the Volunteers.

Kilmainham Jail, which had been closed, was reopened to intern those arrested for their part in the Rising. Of the hundreds arrested after the Rising many were interned in Ballykinlar, Co. Down, and in Frongoch concentration camp in Wales. It was here that the plans for the reorganised Irish Volunteers were laid. The Military Staff of the I.R.B. internees, under the Camp Commandant and Adjutant, W.J. Brennan-Whitmore, developed Frongoch from an internment camp into a Military Academy for the prisoners. They were given full liberty by the camp authorities to parade, drill and conduct military lectures within the camp. Because they expected to be interned until the war ended the officers and men were confident that, on their release, the nucleus of a trained army would return to Ireland. However, most were released after seven months under the General Release of prisoners in December 1916. When they and the internees from Ballykinlar were released they returned to their parishes throughout the country and immediately re-joined their old Volunteer companies and they set about forming Volunteer Companies where none had previously existed.

Patrick Pearse

1917

Throughout this year, drilling and training under the influence of the Irish Republican Brotherhood was being carried out in West Cork as it was throughout the rest of the country. Drilling and instuction were carried out on two or three nights each week within Company areas. These meetings were held in private houses or in a local hall. Lectures on firearms, explosives and military tactics were delivered at these gatherings, and a route march of ten or twelve miles was undertaken each Sunday. Often these marches would be into another Company area or would be undertaken in conjunction with an adjoining Company, with the object of becoming totally familiar with the terrain. This practice was to serve the Volunteers well in 1920-21 when so many of them had to go "on the run."

Lloyd George, as a result of pressure from the United States and some Dominion governments, now summoned a convention to settle the Irish question. The convention was just a window-dressing exercise to persuade President Wilson of America that England was seriously trying to resolve the Irish question. Mr. Page, the American ambassador to England, was advocating Home Rule for Ireland at this time.

Arthur Griffith, writing in the "Nation" (June 2nd. 1917), said "Mr. Lloyd George summons a convention, it is to assure the world that England left the Irish to settle the question of Government themselves and that they could not agree."

Dr. Walsh, Archbishop of Dublin, in his Lenten Pastoral, said "Though I direct you to pray for it, I know that this Convention has no authority from the Irish people."

Cardinal Manning addressing Llyod George, said, "I am convinced that we hold Ireland by force, not only against the will of the majority but in violation of all rights, natural and supernatural, of political justice and religous concience."

The Convention was meant to fail as far as Ireland was concerned, and fail it did.

The first Volunteer Convention since the Easter Rising was held in October 1917. Eamonn De Valera was elected President of the Irish Volunteers and Michael Collins, leader of the I.R.B., was elected to the Executive Council of the Volunteers. He was appointed Director of Organisation and immediately set about re-organising all the old Volunteer Companies and forming new Companies until there was a Volunteer Company in almost every parish in the country. He had the responsibility, as Adjutant - General, of ensuring that a proper system of command existed in each Company area, establishing lines of communications and seeing that training in arms was provided. It was about this time also that an Intelligence Department was created and in a very short while Collins had infiltrated Dublin Castle, the bastion of British rule in Ireland.

CONSCRIPTION AND THE CONSEQUENCES.

1918

The war with Germany had not been going well for England. Her losses of manpower in France were huge in 1917, 250,000 men lost in two months. Replacements were urgently required. Although the British Government had excluded Ireland from the 1916 Conscription Bill the decision was now taken to introduce conscription to Ireland by an Order in Council.

At a Cabinet debate in May 1918, Neville Chamberlain pointed out that the reason why it was proposed to apply conscription to Ireland was, "that the issue of compulsion had been raised and the Nationalists had replied with a direct challenge to the unity of the Empire. To withdraw from compulsion was to surrender unity." he said.

Although the Irish Parliamentary Party under Redmond had, from 1914, exhorted Irishmen to join the British Army in the belief that Lloyd George would deliver Home Rule for Ireland after the war against Germany was won, when the Conscription Bill became law in April 1918 it was not supported by them. They returned to Ireland forthwith and were represented by John Dillon and Joe Devlin at the Mansion House Conference, which was convened on April 18th. An Anti-Conscription Pledge was issued from that Conference, along with a declaration denying the right of the British

David Lloyd George

Government to impose compulsory military service in this country against the clear wishes of the people.

The immediate result of the threat to introduce conscription was a huge increase in the ranks of the volunteers. The country was determined to resist conscription by every means possible. Young and old joined the Volunteers; political differences were forgotten in the face of this threat. The need for weapons took on a new urgency. The I.R.B. instructed all Companies to secure all the arms and ammunition they could in each

16

area. Some arms were given voluntarily but many raids were carried out by the individual Volunteer Companies on private houses and on places suspected of having, or known to have, arms or explosives such as quarries, lighthouses and County Council magazines.

March 1918

It was on St. Patrick's Day of this year that the first raid on an R.I.C. Barracks was carried out. Each Volunteer Company realised that any arms that they hoped to get could only be got locally and those who had the arms were the R.I.C. and the occupation forces So they turned their attention towards the R.I.C. Barracks, of which there was one in almost every village.

In the village of Eyeries, on the Beara penninsula, the R.I.C. Barracks was manned by a Sergeant and three Constables. On St. Patrick's Day, March 17th., there was a Volunteer Parade from Eyeries to Castletownbere which the Sergeant, with one Constable, decided to follow in order to take note of those participating in the parade. This left only two men in the Barracks at Eyeries. Some Volunteers saw this as a golden opportunity to raid for the arms held there and Christy O'Connell (later a Section Commander at the Battle of Crossbarry) along with Sean O'Driscoll, Peter O'Neill, Joe Foley and Con O'Dwyer seized this opportunity.

Their plan, which had to be carried out before the Sergeant and his Constable returned, was quite simple. One of the raiders would knock at the door of the Barracks and, imitating the voice of the Sergeant request that the door be opened, whereupon the Volunteer would produce his gun and followed by the other four overpower the two Constables in charge. Of the raiding party, O'Connell had a revolver with two bullets and O'Driscoll and Foley each had a revolver, also with two or three bullets. Christy O'Connell went around to the front of the building while the others remained out of sight by the gable. Before he could approach the door, to his surprise, he was confronted by an equally surprised Constable who had just stepped out of the building. O'Connell immediately aimed his gun at the man and ordered him to raise his hands above his head. The constable made a threatning move with what O'Connell thought was a gun in his hand and he fired twice at him but the gun misfired. The Constable ran to the door, but before he could close it he was bowled over as O'Connell flung himself at him and they both ended up in the hallway of the Barracks. The other Volunteers on hearing the commotion rushed in and overpowered the Constable. They expected to find two Constables in the Barracks but the second man had left earlier and their prisoner was the only Constable on duty. They gathered up all the arms and ammunition in the building and left the unfortunate man to report their action to his Sergeant on the latter's return from Castletownbere.

Lloyd George now abandoned any attempt to introduce conscription. All that had been achieved by the threat of conscription was to stimulate Sinn Fein and Ireland's claim for national independence. Ireland was roused and the historian, A.J.P. Taylor (English History, 1914 to 1945) said "This was the decisive moment at which Ireland ceded from the Union of Great Britain and Ireland."

May 1918
Britain now purported to have discovered a German plot (never substantiated) and arrested Eamonn de Valera, Arthur Griffith, and about 150 other Sinn Fein officers. A wave of sympathy for Sinn Fein swept throughout the country.

Eamonn de Valera

Michael Collins

1918
On American Independence Day, July 4th 1918, President Wilson stated that all questions about independence and political relations should be based on "the free acceptance of the settlement by the people concerned" and not based on "the advantage of any other people which may desire a

different settlement for the sake of it's own mastery. We seek the reign of law based on the consent of the governed".

On that same 4th of July 1918, President Wilson's English allies, declared illegal, the Gaelic League, the G.A.A., Sinn Fein and the Irish Volunteers. All meetings, assemblies and processions were banned. Hurling and Football matches could be played only after a permit had been granted by the authorities.

In defiance of this ban, on Sunday August 4th. 1918, one thousand five hundred hurling and football matches were played throughout Ireland.

Martial Law was declared in four counties viz: Cork, Limerick, Kerry and Tipperary and the wholesale arrests of leaders of the Volunteers, Sinn Fein and other groups in each parish were attempted by the British but many of these men were now "On the run" and through the support of the people, now united behind the Volunteers, they evaded arrest.

Martial Law is defined as the suspension of ordinary law (courts and trial by jury etc) and the government of a country, or parts of it, by Military Tribunal.

The First Dáil Eireann

THE FIRST DÁIL

November 1918

When World War 1 came to an end on the 11th of November 1918 the conscription scare also came to an end and many of those who had joined the Volunteers since April 16th. now left the organisation. Those who remained were of the right calibre.

1918

World War 1 was over. The Allies were victorious. Britain was now determined to deal with Ireland once and for all, by every means in its power.

The British Parliament was dissolved on November 25th 1918 and Lloyd George called general elections in Great Britain and Ireland to be held on December 14th 1918.

Sinn Fein were delighted as they saw this as an opportunity to test the mood of the people towards their organisation. They put forward 105 canditates to contest seats throughout the country.

There was a problem in Ulster in that the seats there would be contested by the Irish Parliamentary Party and Sinn Fein, thus splitting the Nationalist vote and consequently giving the Unionists the opportunity of winning all of the eight Ulster constituencies. To prevent this happening, Cardinal Logue was asked to conciliate between the Irish Party and Sinn Fein. The outcome was what became known as the "Logue Pact" whereby each of the two parties contested only four seats each. The seats allocated to Sinn Fein were in stong Unionist areas but they won three of the four seats. The final result in Ulster was: Unionists; 23 seats. Sinn Fein; 10 seats. Irish Parliamentary Party: 5 seats. In 24 of the 32 counties, the people elected only Sinn Fein candidates.

Over the whole country Sinn Fein won 73 of the 105 seats they had contested and were now the largest Nationalist party in the country. The Irish Parliamentary Party, John Redmond's Party, was virtually wiped out.

There were now 73 Sinn Fein M.P.s elected to the British Parliament at Westminster all of whom refused to take their seats in that Parliament. The result of the election was a clear decision of the people denying the right of the British Government to govern Ireland.

Dáil Éireann, January 1919

Front Row (L to R): J. O'Doherty, J. Hayes, J.J. O'Kelly, Count Plunkett, Cathal Brugha, Seán T. O'Kelly, P. Ó Máille, J.J. Walsh, T. Kelly. *Second Row:* J. Sweeney, K. O'Higgins, D. Buckley, P. Ward, P.J. Moloney, R. Sweetman. *Third Row:* R. Barton, E. Duggan, P. Béaslaí, Doctor J. Ryan, Doctor Crowley, J. Burke. *Back Row:* R. Mulcahy, C. Collins, P. Shanahan.

In their election manifesto Sinn Fein had stood for total independence for Ireland and the establishment of the Irish Republic. They aimed to achieve these goals by:

(a) withdrawing their elected representatives from the British Parliament and by denying the right of, and opposing the will of, the British or any other foreign government, to legislate for Ireland.

(b) using any and every means to render the power of England to hold Ireland in subjection, by military force or otherwise, impossible.

The people voted overwhelmingly for just that. Sinn Fein had their mandate from the people.

1919

The Sinn Fein members now met for the first time on 21st. January 1919 in the Mansion House in Dublin. At this meeting only 28 of the 73 elected members could attend as 36 were in jail and some others were in America trying to gain support for Ireland's cause. Cathal Brugha was elected Ceann Comhairle and a provisional constitution was adopted.

This was the First Dáil.

The 1916 Declaration of the Irish Republic was ratified:

Whereas the Irish Republic was proclaimed in Dublin on Easter Monday 1916 on behalf of the Irish people and the Irish electorate has in the General Election of 1918, seized the first occasion to declare, by an overwhelming majority, it's firm allegiance to the Irish Republic, we the elected representatives ratify the establishment of the Irish Republic.

In a message to the nations of the world they stated,

Ireland is one of the most ancient nations in Europe and she has preserved her national integrity, vigorous and intact, through seven centuries of foreign oppression; she has never relinquished her national rights and, throughout the long era of English occupation, she has, in every generation, definitely proclaimed her inalienable right of nationhood down to her last glorious resort to arms in 1916. Ireland, resolutely and irrevocably determined that she will suffer foreign domination no longer, calls upon every free nation to uphold her national claim to complete independence as an Irish Republic against the arrogant pretensions of England, founded in fraud, and sustained only by an overwhelming military occupation, and demands to be confronted publicly with England at the Congress of Nations that the civilized world, having judged

English wrong and Irish right may guarantee to Ireland it's permanent support for the maintainence of her national independence.

The cover of the historic pronouncement of Irelands Independence January 21st 1919.

After that first meeting of the Dáil, Cathal Brugha was declared President and Sean T. O'Kelly was elected Ceann-Comhairle to replace him. At the next meeting of the Dáil, Cathal Brugha resigned in favour of Eamonn de Valera, whose escape from Lincoln Jail in England, in the meantime, had been engineered by Michael Collins.

From the beginning, de Valera, Brugha, now Minister for Defence, and other Ministers were determined that the Irish Volunteers would become the National Army under the control of the Government.

Speaking at the Sinn Fein Ard Fheis in April 1919, President de Valera said "the Irish Volunteers were Ireland's National Army and they now had a National Government behind them and no further moral sanction was needed.They had placed themselves at the disposal of the elected Government of the Irish people. They would stand by that Government of the Irish Nation and would do exactly as the Government commanded them."

It was agreed on the 19th August 1919 that an Oath of Allegience to the Republic should be sworn by each member of the Dáil, its officials and the Army.

Thus the Irish Volunteers became the Irish Republican Army (the I.R.A.) under the control of the elected government of the people of Ireland.

The Dáil was a source of legimate authority. It was the symbol of resistance. It enabled men to fight against the British as soldiers of an elected Government, not as rebels (or terrorists as the British called them). The military headquarters staff had the authority of the Minister for Defence and they directed the fight against the Royal Irish Constabulary, the British occupation forces, the Black and Tans and latterly, the Auxiliaries.

1919
We now had two Governments in Ireland:
(a) The Government overwhelmingly elected by the people of Ireland, called Dáil Eireann.
(b) The British Government, claiming jurisdiction over Ireland and enforcing that claim by force of arms.

THE FORMATION OF THE THIRD CORK BRIGADE

1919

Prior to the formation of Cork No. 3 Brigade (later on, better known as the West Cork Brigade) in early 1919, all Volunteer Companies in County Cork and Cork City were controlled by what was known as Cork County Brigade, there being then only one Brigade in the whole county. It became obvious to Tomas Mac Curtain, the Commanding Officer of the Brigade and his fellow Officers that the Brigade area was geographically too large and the number of Volunteer Companies too numerous, to be effectively controlled and adminstered by one Brigade Staff. It was decided to dissolve the original Cork County Brigade and in its stead form three new ones.

Now the county was divided into three Brigade areas:
1. Cork No.1 Brigade: Cork City and Mid Cork, commanded by Tomas Mac Curtain.
2. Cork No.2 Brigade: North and North East Cork, Commanded by Liam Lynch.
3. Cork No.3 Brigade: West Cork, from Innishannon to Castletownbere, Commanded by Tom Hales.

A meeting (presided over by Michael Collins, G.H.Q. Dublin) of staff oficers of the six Battalions existing in West Cork was held at Kilnadur on January 5th 1919. This was the formation of the Third Cork Brigade.

The six Battalions that existed in West Cork: Bandon (1st Batt.), Clonakilty (2nd Batt.), Dunmanway (3rd Batt.), Skibbereen (4th Batt), Bantry (5th Batt.) and Beara (6th Batt.), were all fused into one Brigade The Third Cork Brigade. The Schull Battalion (7th Batt.) was formed in July 1920.

The Brigade Staff Officers elected were: Tom Hales, O.C.; Hugh Thornton, Vice O.C.; Michael Mc Carthy, Adjutant; Denis O'Shea, Quartermaster.; Denis O'Connell, Intelligence Officer.

It was at this stage that the history of the Volunteer Movement in West Cork became the history of The Third Cork Brigade, or, as it was to become more popularly known, "The West Cork Brigade." (see "Towards Ireland Free." by Liam Deasy).

Immediately arrangements were made to perfect the Brigade communications and intelligence systems. In each Battalion area a few sound sympathisers were approached for the purpose of having their adresses used for the receipt of dispatches from Brigade Headquarters

(Bandon) per post. In Bandon similar covering adresses were used to receive dispatches from General Headquarters Dublin and from each of the other Battalions in the Brigade area. In all cases sympathisers whose addresses were used were not previously to have come under enemy notice thus ensuring a certain degree of security. At times of course during raids the enemy secured the name of a covering address. When this happened Brigade Headquarters were immediately notified and the necessary changes were made. Eventually this covering address system had to be abandoned and alternative lines of communications established.

Almost overnight a change had to be made and with scarcely the loss of a few hours a much more efficient system was established by securing a chain of Railway workers (Engine Drivers, Fireman, Checkers, Porters) throughout West Cork. With this system dispatches leaving Bandon by the evening train going West were delivered in all six Batallion Headquarters the same evening. This also applied to dispatches Eastward bound for Bandon. It must be remembered that in this period enemy Intelligence Policemen were specially on the lookout at all Rail stations for any I.R.A. men travelling or otherwise and this most successful communication system operated under their noses.

On September 10th 1919 nine months after the first meeting at the Mansion House and the ratification of the 1916 Declaration, the Dáil was declared illegal by the British Government.

Through the propaganda issued by the Dáil offices and through envoys sent abroad, the world knew of Dáil Eireann and when the British Government declared it to be illegal, they were outlawing the representatives of Ireland who had been elected under British Law, by the people of Ireland, in the election called by the British Government in December 1918.

So in 1919 the first fruits of the 1916 Easter Rising were realised.

Ireland had her own democratically elected Government, her own Army (albeit a guerilla army) and during this period, the administative departments of that Government were put in place. Republican Courts were set up and functioned throughout the country with, not only criminal cases but civil cases being heard, and with the verdicts of these courts being accepted by the people. Emissaries were dispatched to various countries. The ordinary citizen saw Irish institutions functioning more and more throughout the land. But Ireland needed to secure a hearing at the Peace Conference now about to take place in Europe.

The American Congress passed a resolution by 261 votes to 41 that the Peace Conference should consider Ireland's claim to a hearing favourably but President Wilson, (who once said "Ireland is a millstone around my neck") allowed himself to be outwitted by Lloyd George, who had secured the agreement of the four great powers that no claim could be heard at the Conference without the approval of each of the four powers. England most certainly did not approve of Ireland's claim to self determination.

1919

It was early in this year also that a National Loan was launched by the new Dáil to raise £250,000, the collection of which fell on the Irish Volunteers and the Sinn Fein clubs. The public response was such that the amount collected was £379,000. The funds collected were deposited safely throughout the country without the locations being known to the police, who were authorised to seize them.

R.I.C. Barracks in Bandon

The Royal Irish Constabulary (R.I.C.) were the Police Force in the country and they served the British Government well. They were nearly all Irishmen and were the eyes and ears of the Crown Forces in Ireland.There was an R.I.C. barracks in almost every village throughout the country.They knew the activities of every family in their area. Up to

1917 they had concerned themselves with their ordinary police duties but now they informed the military of the names of I.R.A. members and sympthatisers, and even those who attended I.R.A. members' funerals. They led the military on raids on the homes of I.R.A. men where they very often ransacked the houses and mistreated the occupants.

R.I.C. Members from a captured photograph album.

Most of them did everything they could to foil the activities of the Volunteers.They harassed the families of the Volunteers and the neighbours who they thought might be sympathetic towards the Republican cause. Some of them had notebooks in which they entered the names and physical details of Volunteers. One such notebook is in the possession of the author and the information contained in it on individual Vounteers is quite remarkable.There were some few members of the R.I.C. who were sympathetic to the cause of Irish freedom and would inform the Volunteers of an impending raid. Prior to their change of attitude towards the people they had been a respected Police Force. Now, in 1919, they were ostracised and very effectively boycotted by the people in favour of Sinn Fein police.They could no longer be the "eyes and ears" of the British Government .

In December 1919, Lloyd George with all party support, introduced in the House of Commons a "Bill for the Better Government of Ireland".The Bill provided for separate Parliaments in the six north-eastern counties and the other twenty six counties, giving them autonomy only in domestic matters under the supreme control of Westminister. A Council of Ireland was to be set up by these domestic Parliaments which was to have control of certain matters of national concern. They were empowered, if they so agreed, to re-unite the country under a single Parliament.Even though the Bill proposed to grant Ireland more powers of self- government than Gladstone had proposed, it received no support whatsoever outside of Ulster. Anyway, after 1916, Home Rule for Ireland was out of date. Ireland wanted freedom and self-determination and nothing else would do.

On the 15th October, at a meeting of General Headquarters Staff, the decision to hold a National Convention of the Volunteers in December was announced. All Brigades throughout the country were to be represented. Each Brigade Commander was to call a meeting, with representation from each Company, to discuss the decision of the Volunteer Executive to transfer the Volunteer organisation to the control of Dáil Eireann under the title of the Irish Republican Army.

By the end of 1919, Michael Collins had a communications organisation built up throughout the entire country that embraced the postal workers, the railway workers, the dock workers, members of the R.I.C. and others. The postal workers provided highly confidential information gleaned from communications adressed to the local army and police chiefs, while his contacts within the R.I.C. often supplied him with the police codes in use at the time. The information thus procured was very often transported by the engine drivers and guards on the railway network to the local Volunteer Companies. The dockers enabled supplies procured abroad to enter the country without inspection and enabled members of the Dáil, who were going abroad to solicit support for Ireland's cause, to leave the country unnoticed. In May 1920, the dockers together with the railway workers, refused to handle military supplies for the British knowing that they were to be used against their fellow Irishmen.

In the Post Office here in Bandon there was a young lady, Miss May Twomey, who organised her fellow workers and who would, each morning, intercept any mail adressed to the local military and R.I.C. She would hand it over to the I.R.A. Brigade Intelligence Officer, Sean Buckley, or his assistant. They would steam open the envelopes, note the contents, re-seal and return the mail to Miss Twomey who would see that it was delivered, with the second daily delivery, to whom it was adressed.

The information gained in this way was obviously invaluable to the organisation and dispatch riders would cycle throughout the Brigade area to inform the local Company Captains of the information gained in this way. The risk that this young woman took each day could easily have led to her imprisonment or death. There were many like her up and down the country during the War of Independence. The "Black and Tans" and later the "Auxiliaries" did not often discriminate between male and female in their treatment of the Irish people.

On one occassion a vital piece of information gained in this way was to prove prophetic for one Brigade officer. In January 1920 a letter adressed to the British Commanding Officer for West Cork was intercepted. It was to inform him that a major round-up of the "rebels" in West Cork was to be undertaken . Furthermore, once arrested, they were to be shipped to England, without trial, and incarcerated in Wormwood Scrubs Prison (London), which was being cleared out for this purpose. This information was sent to Michael Collins in Dublin who immediately ordered that all Company Captains in the West Cork area should be warned.

He ordered the Volunteer officer who was the first to know of the proposed round-up to cycle from Kinsale to Castletownbere to inform each Company Captain in the Brigade area. For security reasons Collins felt that the Company Captains should be verbally informed.The Volunteer Officer set off on this long journey and, having completed his task, returned home to Bandon. A short time later, on the 1st January 1920, he was surprised by the enemy and arrested; he was shipped to England and lodged in Wormwood Scrubs Prison. It is surely ironic, that being the first to know of the planned round-up, he was also among the first group to be jailed in the "Scrubs".

Those interned in Wormwoods Scrubbs were denied privileges to which they were entitled under the printed rules of the prison and they went on hunger-strike. After days without eating they were removed from the prison to hospitals in London where they were treated under military guard. During their period in hospital they managed, by many different ruses, to obtain large numbers of hospital visitor passes and it was arranged that on a particular Sunday they would each be visited by a number of sympathisers living in England. These visitors arrived with articles of civilian clothing hidden about their persons. When each prisoner had the required number of visitors, he quietly dressed himself in the civilian clothes. When visiting time was up it was found, to the immense consternation of the military guards and hospital staff, that all the prisoners had walked out as visitors. The following morning the prisoners read the news of themselves on the billboards outside newsagents and stations "100 wild Irishmen loose in London". My father, who was among these "100" wild Irishmen, told me that to listen to the comments and fears of the Londoners one would think that they were talking about gorillas. Hence, they were able to mix among these Londoners, completely unsuspected, until they could make their way back to Ireland.

Photograph of volunteers taken after the hunger-strike in Wormwood Scrubs, London in 1920.
Back row, (L to R): Paddy Crowley, Kilbrittain Company ; Dan Canty, Captain Newcestown Company ; Flor Begley, Adjutant Bandon Company and later Assistant Brigade Adjutant. *Front row (L to R):* Felix Cronin, Lorrha, Co. Tipperary; Miss Egan, London; Pat O' Leary Captain Kilmurray Company.

THE BRITISH TERROR POLICY INCREASES

Events progressed very rapidly from late 1919. Lloyd George was determined to enforce British rule in Ireland by whatever means were required to do so. In the House of Commons on December 1919 he said: "any attempt at secession will be fought with the same determination, with the same resources, with the same resolve as the Northern States of America put into the fight against the Southern States. It is important that this should be known not merely throughout the world, but in Ireland itself." His chief advisor Sir Henry Wilson, who was ardently pro-Ulster exhorted him to use the greatest force at his disposal. The Chief Secretary of Ireland Macpherson, a moderate Home Ruler, was frustrated by the introduction of Lloyd George's Government of Ireland Act and resigned.

During late 1919, the Third Cork Brigade was chiefly involved in training and in procuring arms and ammunition. After the attack by Dan Breen on the R.I.C. at Soloheadbeg in County Tipperary (often looked upon as the beginning of the War of Independence) I.R.A. Headquarters in Dublin had given permission to the Brigade to attack R.I.C Barracks and Coastguard Stations to capture arms and also to force the R.I.C. to abandon the smaller outposts, thus removing the "eyes and ears" of the British Government and making large areas safe for the Volunteers. Training camps and rest camps were then set up in these areas for those Volunteers "on the run".

An attack on the Barracks in Allihies heralded in this new development in activities in the Brigade area. (see "Towards Ireland Free", by Liam Deasy).

On the 1st January 1920, the twelve Companies in the 1st Battalion of the Third Cork Brigade, were most efficiently organised. Many of the men in these Companies had endured various terms of imprisonment, or were on the run previously during the years leading up to 1920, a fact which considerably strengthened the morale of each Company and gave inspiration and courage to others who had not been imprisoned or otherwise knocked about. At this time enemy activity became more intensive and aggressive so much so that hardly a man in the Battalion escaped attention in some form or another, either through raids on the family home or through being intercepted during the day or night and being subjected to many indignities.

Just to be a member of any of the Irish organisations, the Gaelic League, G.A.A., Sinn Fein etc. (declared banned organisations by the

British on 4th July 1918), was enough to attract undue attention and harassment from the Police and the Army.

1920

The year of the Murder Gangs. The year of the "Black and Tans", the "Auxies" and the Essex "Torture Squad". The year of the murder of Tomas Mac Curtain, the Burning of Cork, the indiscriminate shooting of players and spectators at the Football match in Croke Park on Bloody Sunday, the Destruction of Mallow, the Sack of Fermoy. The list of atrocities perpetrated in the name of the Crown in 1920 goes on and on. It was the most important year in the War of Independence.

The Dáil had been declared illegal and met only very infrequently as most of its members were either in jail or "on the run" but the republican newspapers, known as the "Mosquito Press", reported on the Dáil and its activities thus establishing it in the minds of the people as the legitimate and only Government of Ireland. Meanwhile the local Volunteer Company with its Police Force, Courts, its visible fighting force and declared allegiance to the Dáil, was very real in the community.

In January 1920, Urban and Municipal Elections were held throughout the country and these were the first test for the people who had returned Sinn Fein candidates in the General Election of December 1918.

The difference between the elections of 1920 when compared with the radio and television coverage of elections today is hard to imagine. In the 1920 elections, to be caught by the police with election pamphlets supporting Republican candidates was regarded as treason against the British Empire and warranted imprisonment without trial. For the election, Britain introduced P.R.(proportial representation) for the first time in the hope of avoiding defeat for the Loyalist candidates. The people however, once again, voted overwhelmingly for the Sinn Fein candidates and, in almost every city and town, Sinn Fein and Labour between them controlled the Councils.

In Cork, Tomas Mac Curtain was elected Lord Mayor and other Sinn Fein council members were elected Lords Mayor in other cities throughout the country.

On April 4th 1920 Sinn Fein raided Tax Offices all over the country and destroyed all the records found in them. The result of this was that the British Adminstration could no longer collect revenue except through Customs and Excise.

In May 1920 there were 47 instances of the sacking, burning or bombing of towns and villages and in the first week of July there were six killed, seven attempted murders, sixteen woundings and eighteen sackings, burnings or bombings.(The "Irish Bulletin" July 20th 1920). All of this was done by the forces of law and order.

On June 5th 1920 it was reported in that same newspaper that W.Long M.P. said in Westminster "the Police have not only shot, but they have shot with extremly good effect and he only hoped that they do it again". Also in June Crown forces looted and wrecked thirty five shops in Fermoy as a reprisal for the capture of General Lucas by the I.R.A.

When the elections for the County and Rural District Councils were held in June 1920, the results were the same resulting in almost every Council in the country being under the control of Sinn Fein. The Councils now ignored the orders and recommendations of the Local Government Board (the British Local Authority) and regarded the recommendations and orders of the Dáil as the legitimate instructions of Government. On Sept 30th 1920, all the Councils made a clean break with the British Local Government Board.

The Dáil was now the only legitimate authority in the country accepted by the people. The ideals of Easter Week were being realised. But, before the collapse of British rule in Ireland was to be acheived after 700 years, the British Government introduced a reign of terror and oppression never before seen here with the introduction of murder gangs with "carte blanche" and complete and guaranteed exemption from legal sanctions. Responsible to no one for their actions, they were the Essex Torture Squad, the Black and Tans and the Auxiliaries. I will deal with each of these "official" terror group0s and some of their activities later on.

On January 27th 1920, the Catholic Bishops of Ireland condemned the Military Rule in Ireland. However, before 1916 the majority of the clergy were supporters of John Redmond's Parliamentary Party and led by Cardinal Logue, most of the bishops either condemned the Rising or made no public comment on it. After the excutions of the leaders and the widespread arrests which followed the Rising, very many of the priests but few of the Hierarchy, supported the cause of freedom and some of them played a very active role in the return of Sinn Fein candidates in subsequent elections and, later, in the War of Independence itself.

By the beginning of 1920 the Volunteers had begun their attacks on some of the more isolated R.I.C. Barracks throughout County Cork forcing the Police to abandon them and to move into the towns. While no lives were lost in these actions the clergy condemned them, despite the fact that the British were carrying out thousands of raids on the homes of their parishioners, in many cases wrecking their homes, mistreating and arresting members of the families. As the War of Independence intensified the clergy still continued to condemn attacks on the R.I.C. and the British Forces. However, having witnessed the actions of the Black and Tans and the Auxiliaries against the ordinary people of their parishes from the summer of 1920 onwards, condemnations from the Bishops and the priests became less frequent. In his book "No Other Law" Florrie O'Donoghue gives his judgement of the situation at the time: "a few individual priests, with truly heroic fortitude, took their stand with the Volunteers, and suffered for it: but on the part of the bishops and the majority of the clergy the reaction to early military activities of the national armed forces was one of unqualified disapproval and condemnation."

As the exesses of the Black and Tans, the Auxiliaries, the Crown Forces and the repression of the nation as a whole became more and more apparent throughout 1920 many more bishops and priests were only too ready to condemn the actions of the British Forces. In a statement of the Irish Hierarchy after its meeting in Maynooth in October 1920 the bishops gave their most forthright indictment of British policy in Ireland when they declared: "On a scale truly appalling have to be reckoned countless indiscriminate raids in the darkness of night, prolonged imprisonments without trial, savage sentences from tribunals that command and deserve no confidence, the burning of houses, town halls, factories, creameries and crops, the destruction of industries to pave the way for famine by men maddened by plundered drink and bent on loot, the floggings and massacre of citizens, all perpetrated by the forces of the Crown who have established a reign of frightfulness, which for murdering the innocent and destroying their property, has a parallel only in the horrors of Turkish atrocities or in the outrages of the Red Army in Bolshevist Russia."

One practical way by which they showed their support for the Volunteers was by their attendance in great numbers at the funerals of victims of the British regime whether they had actively opposed the British rule in Ireland or were innocent victims of the Military policy of reprisals. The Catholic bishops and priests were rarely if ever, raided or harassed by the R.I.C. up to 1920 but with the arrival of the Black and Tans this soon changed and from September 1920 onwards raids on colleges and other Catholic institutions and the searching of priest's houses became commonplace with the subsequent arrest and detention of the priests. Three Cahtolic priests were murdered by the Crown Forces during the War of Independence:

Fr. Michael Griffin of Galway in November 1920.
Canon Magner of Dunmanway. Co. Cork. in December 1920.
Fr. James O'Callaghan of Cork in May 1921.

Wireless Section of British Garrison at Bandon.

THE MURDER OF CORK'S LORD MAYOR

At the beginning of 1920, the entire arsenal of the West Cork Brigade consisted of: 50 rifles, an assortment of shotguns, .22 rifles and revolvers. Following two attacks on the Coastguard Station at Howes Strand and attacks on other enemy posts during the first six months of the year, the arms of the Brigade had increased to 88 rifles, together with shotguns and revolvers, and 27,000 rounds of ammunition.(see "Towards Ireland Free" by Liam Deasy)

Tomás MacCurtain

These rifles and the ammunition had to be hidden from the enemy and in each Company area ammunition dumps had to be maintained. These dumps would have to be dug up every so often, the guns re-cleaned and oiled, and transferred to a newly dug dump. The dumps were disguised in many ways, some times with a cock of hay placed over them, or the weapons might be placed in a potato pit, or buried in a fence. The location and maintainence of the dumps were the responsibility of the local Company. For instance, in the Newcestown Company area there were four large dumps in late 1920 as well as a number of small ones.

Newcestown Company area was regarded as a base for the fitting out of the Brigade Flying Column when this renowned unit was later formed and on average there would be at least 60 rifles, along with some mines, in dumps in this area.

The Brigade Prison, known as the "Black Bog" was also in this Company area.

1920

In the Spring of 1920 the British Government stepped up their campaign of suppression in Ireland.

On March 18th British forces attempted to murder Professor Stockley in Cork. Their first attempt failed and they made a second attempt two days later. This also failed.

On the night of the 20th of March 1920, the R.I.C. went to the home of the newly elected Lord Mayor, Tomas Mac Curtain, and demanded entry. Mrs. Mac Curtain opened the door to them whereupon they pushed past her and murdered her husband in front of her and her five children. A Coroner's inquest found that the Lord Mayor had been brutally murdered and returned a verdict of wilful murder against the R.I.C., Lord French, the Lord Lieutenent of Ireland, and Lloyd George, the Prime Minister of England.

On March 24th the Evening Herald in London informed its readers that "in Ireland the military are running amok".

At a special meeting of Cork Corporation Terence Mac Swiney was elected to succeed his friend and fellow Volunteer as Lord Mayor of Cork. A short time after his appointment the police raided City Hall and he was arrested for having a police code in his office. He was courtmartialed and sentenced to two years imprisonment. He informed the Court that he would not serve the sentence in full. He was taken to Brixton Prison in London, 12th August 1920. In protest he went on hunger-strike which lasted 74 days ending in his death on October 25th 1920. The nations of the world were appalled that England had allowed him to die on hunger-strike.

Terence Mac Swiney

On 23rd March, General Sir Nevil Macready was appointed Commander in Chief of the British Armed Forces in Ireland. He arrived in Ireland on 14th April 1920. In his eyes, the Irish were a people "characterized through past centuries by a lack of dicipline, intolerance of restraint, with no common standard of morality and can only be held in check under the protection of a strong military garrison".

His opinion would appear to have been shared by some members of the House of Commons. Mr Bonar Law,leader of the Conservative Party, regarded the Irish as "an inferior race. Even if not regarded as squalid thugs who murdered soldiers on dark nights the Sinn Feiners could scarcely be regarded as leaders. In what sense had present Ireland ever produced leaders?".(White hall Diaries by Tom Jones. Oxford University Press 1971)

Another member, Mr Balfour, said "that it was only a geographical accident that Ireland was surrounded by the sea. This should be ignored

Lord French, Lord Lieutenant of Ireland, and General Macready,
Commander-in-Chief, review their troops.

and their (the Irish) inveterate religous and racial prejudices recognised, on any other line an Irish settlement was a pure illusion". He also suggested that the new powers which would be available under the Criminal Justice Administration Bill (which roughly followed the Defense of the Realm Act) should be confined to districts where they were really required as the powers were the most violent conceivable.

British Ministers saw Irish aspirations to independence in the same light as tribal revolt in India or the Boer rebellion in South Africa. Winston Churchill compared Sinn Fein with the Wafd Party in Egypt, and even Smuts for all his anti-British past, thought the Irish leaders small men living with dreams.(C.P.Scott Diary, Ed.Trevor Wilson, London1970).

There were also those who could not endorse these opinions. William Watson an English poet said, "It is not with self-flattery on our lips - it is with the sackcloth of humility on our backs and with the ashes of contrition on our heads that we English should set about the work of cancelling, as far as may now be possible, the iniquity of more than seven centuries in Ireland. Ireland was asking for independence, a thing she possessed until we took it from her."

Lord Buckmasters daughter in her "Recantation" wrote: My country, England, agreed publically to the principle that "the interest of the weakest is as sacred as the interest of the strongest". Ireland is the test of our sincerity. Not only was I strongly opposed to Sinn Fein during the war (1914-1918) but I acquiesced in the shooting of the rebels after Easter Week (1916 Rising) and was willing to see conscription applied to Ireland. Of these opinions, formed in ignorance, I am now heartily ashamed. England should deal with the fundamental justice of Ireland's claim rather than with the iniquity and futility of adminstration in Ireland where once more was being enacted the oldest of struggles in the defence of the first of rights - Sinn Fein, (We ourselves).

In May 1920 General Tudor was appointed to take over the control and reorganisation of the R.I.C. He brought with him an officer, Colonel Winter, for the sole purpose of the re-organisation of the moribund Intelligence Branch.

May 6th 1920 marked the arrival in Dublin of the newly appointed Chief Secretary of Ireland, Sir Hamar Greenwood. After the British Cabinet had agreed to raise a special force of 8,000 men for the purpose, he immediately set about the task of strengthening the R.I.C. and, as recruits for that Force could no longer be found in Ireland, a special recruiting office was set up in Scotland Yard in London.

General H.H. Tudor

Owing to a shortage of R.I.C. uniforms these recruits were fitted out with khaki army uniforms and with the dark green hats and black belts of the R.I.C. Because of their black and khaki unforms they became known as the "Black and Tans", a name never to be forgotten in Ireland. Later, according to Gen. Macready, Commander in Chief of the Armed Forces in Ireland, these Black and Tans took the law into their own hands, disregarding the R.I.C. and the regular Army Commands and "gave cause for anxiety, both to the Government and to those responsible for the Force".

As policemen they were useless, with a total lack of knowledge of the locality or its inhabitants but, as uncontrolled perpetrators of terror and brutality they had no equal, that is, until the arrival of the Auxiliaries.

The following verse was one that was much favoured among the Black and Tans around this time.

Said Lloyd George to Macpherson, "I'll give you the sack,
To manage old Ireland you haven't the knack.
I'll send over Greenwood, he's a much stronger man,
and we'll fill up the Green Isle with the bold Black and Tans
He sent them all over, to pillage and loot,
To burn down houses and inmates to shoot,
To reconquer Ireland" says he "is my plan
With Macready and Co. and his bold Black and Tans."

The arrival of the "bold Black and Tans" heralded a new phase of the War of Independence. Here was a force that soon, was to be completely out of control.

At this stage also the arrival of additional transport vehicles for the military meant that they became more mobile and could conduct raids on suspected I.R.A.houses with increasing frequency. These raids, of which there were 10,000 in six months and on which the military and the Black and Tans were accompanied by the R.I.C. who directed them to the homes of the suspects, were terrifying visits. In the I.R.A. 1st Battilion (Bandon) area, the Auxiliaries used to join the Police in raids and the destruction of property and the punishment meted out to those in the houses, men, women and youngsters, was brutal in the extreme.

The doors were burst open with rifle butts and the inhabitants rounded up, with blows and kicks, to be questioned. If the answers forthcomng were not to their liking then the troops and "Tans" would further abuse their prisoners, wreck the property, and in many, many cases, set the outhouses or the dwelling on fire. One such Company of Black and Tans. ("K" Company), was typical of that force. They were involved in the burning of Cork City in December 1920.

To counteract the increased mobility of the British Forces and their continuing raiding, the Volunteers resorted to the trenching of roads, the destruction of bridges and the felling of trees across roads. The roads of that time would today be called narrow dirt roads. The following extract from the Farnivane Company Records will illustrate the work involved in road-trenching:

The trenching of roads entailed the employment of numerous horses and carts for the removal of the material raised from the trench and the transportation of same to a location approximately five or six hundred yards away from the trench, thus denying the enemy the opportunity of re-filling it easily. The cutting of each trench necessitated the mobilisation of the entire Company from dusk to dawn, squads of men being engaged as armed protection parties, scouts, carters, pick and shovel men. Men of the Company commandeered horses and carts when required. As this type of work could not be carried out quietly, those involved were in imminent danger of being surprised by enemy patrols, even with scouts posted. In an adjacent Company area four volunteers engaged in such work were surprised and shot by the enemy. In the Ballinadee Company area, members of that Company who were engaged in wrecking the "Long Bridge" over the River Bandon at Kinsale were also surprised by Crown Forces and narrowly escaped being annihilated.

The Farnivane Company records state that trenches were cut in that area as follows:

Gurteen road, Bandon - Crookstown - Macroom, trenched in two places 15ft. x 10ft. x 9ft.
Roughgrove road:	20ft.	wide	x	10ft.	deep	x	10ft. long.
Derrycool road:	23ft.	"	x	12ft.	"	x	12ft. ".
Farnalough road:	20ft.	"	x	9ft.	"	x	10ft. ".
By-road (Newcestown-Mallowgaten)	15ft.	"	x	9ft.	"	x	12ft. ".
Castlelack road:	20ft.	"	x	10ft.	"	x	12ft. ".

(Re-opened and re-trenched 3 times)

The same records state that bridges destroyed in that area were:

Gurteen bridge:	24ft.	"	x	10ft.	"	x	20ft. ".

(Re-opened and destroyed 3 times)

Roughgrove bridge:	25ft.	"	x	8ft.	"	x	20ft. ".

(Re-opened and destroyed twice)

Mallowgaton bridge:	24ft.	"	x	8ft.	"	x	15ft. ".

(Re-opened and destroyed 5 times)

To overcome the trenching the Crown Forces at first carried heavy planks to enable them to cross the trenches, then as the trenches were dug wider this practice was discontinued. As the arrival of more transport in late 1920 enabled the enemy to increase even further the number of raids they carried out, so the trenching of roads in all Company areas was pursued intensively.

SUPPORT FOR THE VOLUNTEERS

By Autumn of 1920, following raids night and day on Volunteers' homes and on the homes of those thought by the British to be sympathetic to the Volunteers, very many men had to leave and go "on the run". These men were now dependent on the ordinary people of the country to feed and shelter them, to supply them with clean socks, underwear, shirts and medical aid. The help they got was unstinting. There were a great number of "safe houses", both in the town and in the country, into which these tired and hungry men were welcomed and fed. One such house was Butlers' of Granfeen. As a consequence of feeding the many Volunteers who called there, the good woman of this house ran up quite a sizable bill for groceries at Jeffers', a Protestant business in Bandon town. The owner of this business, certainly aware that she was purchasing more groceries than she could need for her own family requirements and probably guessing correctly why she needed such supplies, told her not to worry about her account and to take as much time as she wished to settle up. Now this man was not a Nationalist but, like many of the Protestant community he held no brief for the methods now being employed by the British Government to subdue the country.

Another example of the help often forthcoming from the Protestant community involved my father, Flor Begley. He had been laid low by severe influenza, was very weak and was being cared for in Foley's of Castle Road when word came from a sympathetic R.I.C. Sergeant that his presence there had been reported to the Police by an informer. Weak though he was, he made his way out the back of Foley's and up through the "Bogs" to the Park (part of Lord Bandon's estate). He travelled through the trees until he came to Mrs. Bishop's house, the Lodge on the estate, and this kind Protestant lady not alone took him in and put him to bed, but sent for the Doctor and she nursed him back to health over the following. ten days.

The consequences, if caught, of helping or habouring a Volunteer was physical assault, one's house burnt, a prison sentence, or death. Yet, despite this, the people risked everything so great was the desire to be rid of the British. Allied to this desire was the pride, continually growing in the people, in having our own Government, Army, Courts and administration for the first time in 700 years and in the firm belief, that at last, we could be an independent country.

On a lighter note, here is an incident that occured in Mrs. Fitzsimmon's in Shannon St. (now Oliver Plunkett St.) in Bandon.

Fitzsimmons was a grocery shop which also had a liquor licence. The grocery section was towards the front of the shop with a small area towards the rear set aside for the sale of liquor. The shop was quite narrow and at the rear wall, facing the entrance to the shop, was a small bench seat capable of seating just two people. It was on this bench seat that a certain Protestant lady from the street would sit, on occasion, of an evening, and have her little "tot" of whiskey before retiring for the night. In those days shops used to remain open for business until quite late.

Fitzsimmons was one of the "safe houses" in the town and was regularly used by the Officers of the Brigade for short meetings. During these meetings, held in the front room upstairs, Mrs. Fitzsimmons or her sister Miss Bannion, would always take tea and scones up to these men. One night a number of the Volunteers, including Brigade Officers Liam Deasy, Sean Buckley, and Flor Begley, were upstairs when the Military sealed off Shannon Street at both ends and conducted a house to house search for I.R.A Volunteers, arms or incriminating documents. A group of them, led by a Lieutenant, burst into Mrs. Fitzsimmons shop. The Lieutentant ordered his men to search the house from top to bottom. At this point, Miss Gilman, the Protestant lady sitting on the bench at the back of the shop and facing the door (and fully aware that the Volunteers were upstairs and would most certainly be arrested or perhaps killed while trying to escape) raised her glass and in a loud voice said "God save the King". The Lieutenant immediately stopped, came to attention, saluted and said "All right lads, it's obvious that we are in a loyal house, no need to search here" and they left.

Though to many being Protestant meant being loyal to the Crown, this was not necessarily the case at all. One only has to study our history to find many patriots among the Protestant community and I am not referring to the high-profile names like Mc Cracken, Tone or Emmet. Miss Gillman saved the Brigade Officers from certain capture and death that night. There were many such instances throughout the War of Independence in which the Protestant community were involved in helping the Volunteers particularly after the arrival of the Black and Tans and the Auxiliaries.

On the 24th July 1920 a protest of G.W. Biggs of Bantry, a Protestant Unionist, in the "Irish Times" that there was no persecution or intolerance shown by the Republicans in Bantry resulted in his large premises being burned by Crown Forces on 26th July.

It is true that there were many Protestants who considered themselves British and wished to have the connection with Britain and the Empire preserved for ever. Some actively supported the R.I.C and the Military against the legimate army of the Dáil and furnished them with information which often resulted in the capture and sometimes the death of Volunteers. These and their counterparts in the Catholic community were dealt with as spies in any war were dealt with.

Friends in Liverpool, October 1919
(L to R): Reg Dunn, John Phelan (killed at Upton ambush), Jerry O'Sullivan and Peter "Scottie" Monahan (killed at Crossbarry).

THE ARRIVAL OF THE "AUXILIARIES"

In May 1920 Hamar Greenwood told the Cabinet that resignations from the R.I.C. were running at two hundred per week. In July 1920 the following incident occurred at Listowel, Co. Kerry.

Sir Hamer Greenwood inspecting Auxiliaries.

While addressing the men of the Listowel R.I.C. Barracks the newly appointed Divisional Commissioner of Police, Colonel Smyth, insructed them to hand over their barracks to the Military and they would be transferred to other R.I.C. stations throughout Co. Kerry. Colonel Smyth said that the Police would now go on the offensive against the "Shinners" and that they were to patrol the country, lie in ambush, order all civilians to raise their hands and submit to being searched, to shoot them if they were slow in obeying that order and to shoot them if they had their hands in their pockets or in any way seemed to act suspiciously. He assured them that "no policeman would get into trouble for shooting any man".

The fourteen men attached to the barracks refused to obey Smyth and their leader said to him "by your accent I take it that you are English. You forget that you are addressing Irishmen" and taking off his belt and bayonet he threw them on the table and continued, "these too are

English. Take them you murderer." Smyth ordered the others to arrest him but they refused. Colonel Smyth was later shot by the Volunteers at the County Club on the Mall in Cork.

1920

The "Restoration and Maintainence of Order in Ireland Act" which received Royal assent on August 9th1920, abolished trial by jury (too many verdicts of murder were being returned against the Crown forces) and gave the Military administration the power of courtmartial in cases of treason and felony. It replaced coroners inquests by secret military courts of enquiry. These steps proved to be inadequate and on September 3rd 1920 Field Marshal Sir Henry Wilson Chief of the Imperial Military Staff (who was a staunch supporter of Lloyd George's policy of repression and defender of Ulster's right to arm against the South of Ireland) argued for full Government authorisation of reprisals. (Whitehall Diaries, T Jones, Vol 3.)

The lack of her ability to govern Ireland was undermining Britain's image both at home and abroad.Towards the end of the Summer of 1920, the British Cabinet, determined to crush the Volunteers and their supporters, unleashed the worst force of all on the people of Ireland, namely, the Auxiliaries. They were to be an auxiliary police force. The force was made up entirely of ex-British army officers; professional soldiers, battle trained throughout the Empire in the 1914-1918 World War. Many of them could not adjust to civilian life and jumped at the opportunity to return to war, if only against "poorly armed peasants" in "God-forsaken Ireland". They were attached to the R.I.C.. They were to be a special force that was created to terrorize and subdue the Irish quickly. They were to be paid £1 a day. They were not however subject to the control of General Tudor, C. O. of the R.I.C., nor were they subject to the control of General Sir Nevil Macready, C. O. of British Forces in Ireland. No, they were created by Cabinet, were a law unto themselves, and were answerable only to Cabinet.

A more murderous bunch was never before seen in Ireland.

Their Commanding Officer was one Brigadier-General F.P. Crozier C.B, C.M.G., D.S.O. and he had been specially selected as O.C. Auxiliary Division R.I.C.

A brief review of this man's background is appropriate here.

Born in 1879, he was an Anglo-Irish Unionist whose father was a Major in a Scottish Regiment and whose Great-great uncle was Sam Hussey, the "best hated man in the West." He carried out more evictions in Munster than all the other land agents put together. Crozier was an avowed Orangeman and in 1913, he joined the British League for the Defence of Ulster and the Union. He was posted to the West Belfast regiment of the U.V.F.and was given the task of raising a special force of 300 men which was to form a Special Service Section. These men if called out for service were to be paid what they would earn in their jobs in civilian life. Gen. Crozier, in his book "Impressions and Recollections", explains how he was his own clerk, sergeant-major, adjutant, quartermaster and commanding officer, all rolled into one.

Brig. General F.P. Crozier
C.B., C.M.G., D.S.O.

It was a good thing that I was, as one night, in March 1914, I was suddenly told by Colonel Couchman (C.O. of the Belfast District Of the U.V.F.) that I had better go to a certain address to sleep, where I would be available by telephone. I was to register under the name of Percy. When I asked the reason for all this secrecy I was informed that spies (Unionist) in Dublin Castle, administrative Head-quarters of the British in Ireland, had reported that warrants for the arrest of Sir Edward Carson and others, of whom I was probably one, had been issued, and that Sir Edward had left the House of Commons suddenly and dramatically that night and that he would arrive in Belfast the following morning. I was further told that I would have to meet him on the quay with my special service men and escort him to Craigavon, the residence of Captain James Craig.

At the time, I rather doubted the correctness of the statement relative to the issue of a warrant for the arrest of Edward Carson and did not think the Government had the pluck to carry out this very obvious duty (the first duty of a Government being to govern) which in fact was almost the case. I have since been told authoritatively by Lady Aberdeen, whose husband was Lord Lieutenant of Ireland at the time, that a warrant was actually issued, but, that the Government vetoed it's execution, largely on the advice and appeal of John Redmond (leader of the Irish Parliamentary Party in the Commons).

> *If the R.I.C. had attempted to arrest him, a fearful carnage would have ensued, as my orders were quite clear and definite (to prevent the arrest of Carson by the Police) and I would, of course, have carried them out.*

In September 1914, he was appointed Second-in-Command of the 9th. Royal Irish Rifles of the Ulster Division. "This Battalion was really the West Belfast Regiment of Carson's Army under another name" he says, in his book.

With regard to the "Curragh Mutiny" he states that, "Curragh Episode which had so much to do with our fortunes in the North, save to say, that I would do tomorrow what General Gough did then, should I be confronted with a similar situation in any part of the Empire, as the soldiers were asked to do a thing that they should never have been asked to do, namely, to coerce Ulster." (He had no problem with coercing the population in the South later). In the event of conflict with the Forces of the Crown, definite instuctions were issued to him if Sir Edward Carson was to call into being a Provisional Government for the control of Ulster. He was to seize all the R.I.C. Barracks in a certain area and to prevent the military from leaving Victoria Barracks in Belfast at all costs. That he was an able commander is obvious from all of the above. This was the General, specially chosen by the British Cabinet, to command the Auxiliary Division of the R.I.C., the "Auxies".

Macroom Castle where the Auxiliaries were stationed.

1920

The attacks on R.I.C. Barracks, all of which are very well documented in "Towards Ireland Free" by Liam Deasy and "in Guerrilla Days in Ireland" by Tom Barry, continued and the Volunteers of the Third (West) Cork Brigade drove the R.I.C. out of their rural Barracks (remember, there was one in almost every village) into the bigger towns. So thoroughly was this done that by December 1920 the policemen of fifteen R.I.C. Barracks had been forced to abandon them and General Macready claimed that without many more men and extra powers he was unable to control the country.

It was decided at Cabinet on the 9th December 1920 to declare Martial Law in Cork, Kerry, Limerick and Tipperary and the necessary proclamations were issued on the 10th and 12th of that month. These were based on the Martial Law regulations issued by the British during the Boer war in Africa (1899 - 1902).

Martial Law is defined as the suspension of ordinary law (Courts etc.) and the subsequent government of a country, or parts of it, by Military Tribunal.

British politician Neville Chamberlain said "martial law is the abrogation of law".

This was now the case in the aforementioned counties. Permits for all motor vehicles were introduced to deny the Volunteers mobility, and furthermore, bicycles were banned! The Authorities decided that the creameries were the distribution points of orders for the I.R.A. so they were either closed down or burned down by the military.

Fairs and meetings were banned and curfew introduced, firstly, from 9 p.m. to morning, and later from 7 p.m. to morning. Industries and shops were burned so as to create unemployment and thus create further hardship for the people.

In July Winston Churchill felt it was time "to raise the temperature of the conflict to a real issue and shock, and trial of strength". He said he "would at the same time raise 30,000 men in Ulster by whom the authority of the Crown could be vindicated not only in Ulster but throughout Ireland. He would take the seven battalions (regular army) from Ulster for use in the South. He was not afraid of the opposition of the South, because where would they get their arms? He would raise a crisis on the railways and the Post Office. After a raid on a Post Office he would close it. He would stop the subsidy to the railways, shut them up and turn the men off. After three or four days without wages they would want to begin to come to terms." ("Whitehall Diary", Tom Jones).

It must also be remembered that outside the North-Eastern counties the percentage of Loyalists was higher in West Cork than in any other part of the country.

ATROCITIES OF THE AUXILIARIES, THE BLACK AND TANS AND THE ESSEX

I have mentioned that the "Black and Tans" and the Auxiliaries were to subdue the country by all and any means they saw fit. The following details of their actions show just how far they were prepared to go to achieve their goal.

Auxiliaries with civilian as hostage against attack.

On November 1st 1920, Ellen Quinn was deliberately shot dead at Kiltartan, Co. Galway by the Black and Tans. Ellen Quinn was 23 years of age, married and seven months pregnant. When she was fired on by these British Forces she was holding in her arms a baby of nine months. Prior to the murder, there had been no attack on the R.I.C. or any other British Forces in the area. Ellen Quinn was fired on deliberately and was mortally wounded in the abdomen.

The following is a non-republican account of this horrible execution:

The victim of this appalling occurance is Mrs Ellen Quinn of Kiltartan, wife of a popular farmer, and daughter of Mr M. Gilligan of Raheen. She was standing by the stile in front of her house when a lorry of uniformed men passed at a rapid rate. Suddenly, there was a burst of fire and Mrs. Quinn was hit in the right groin, and a number of fowl in the yard were killed. Mrs. Quinn staggered to the door with her baby, which she handed to a servant, and she then collapsed in a pool of blood.

Dr J. Sandys, Gort and Dr Foley, Ardrahan, were quickly on the scene, and Surgeon O'Malley of Galway was telegraphed for but, so great was the terror, that he could not get a motor car to take him to Gort. Eventually, he and Dr Mc Mahon travelled together in the latter's car, only to find that Mrs Quinn had bled to death. Mrs Quinn was in great agony for two hours before she died. She leaves three children the eldest of whom is not yet four years old." (from "The Irish Bulletin", November 1920 and re-produced in the "Kerryman" Christmas Number 1937.).

The Rev John Considine attended Mrs Quinn and this is his account of her death.

"I have heard of Turkish atrocities" he said, "I have read of the death of Joan of Arc. I have read of the sufferings of Nurse Edith Cavell (shot as a spy by the Germans during the 1914 -1918 World War) and as I read I prayed that the good God would change the hearts of the perpetrators, but little did I dream that I should witness a tragedy more cruel than any of these things and that, here, in our own peaceful little parish. My God! it is awful !"

At about 3 p.m., Father Considine added, Malachy Quinn, weeping bitterly, called for him and said that he had just heard that his wife had been shot. Fr. Considine procured a motor car and hurried to the scene. At the gateway there was a large pool of blood on the roadside. Another three yards away in the yard there was another pool, and the porch leading to the kitchen was actually covered in blood. In a room was the poor woman, lying on her back, with blood seeping through her clothes. "Oh! Father John" she said "I have been shot". "Shot by whom?" I exclaimed. "By Police" she answered.

The Kerryman Christmas Number 1937

On December 1st 1920 a group of Auxiliaries almost sacked the town of Fermoy. They were on their way to the funeral of the Auxiliaries killed at Kilmichael a few days before. One of their lorries broke down and they decided to stay in Fermoy until morning. They alighted from their lorries and dispersed to the bars around the town centre where they demanded drink, without payment of course. One group entered the Royal Hotel.

Seated at the bar counter was an ex-British army officer Captain Nicholas Prendergast who had fought in France in the World War. Some altercation arose between the Auxiliaries and him around 11p.m. They accused him of being a supporter of Sinn Fein and dragged him from the hotel on to the Square outside. Here, they beat him up and finally killed him. They then dragged his body to the bridge and threw the remains into the river below.

They returned to the hotel and insisted on holding a dance. The management tried to explain that the neighbours might object to the noise whereupon they left the hotel and proceeded to a premises next door to the hotel and demanded entry. It was the shop and dwelling of a Mr. Dooley. They smashed down the door, dragged Mr. Dooley out, set fire to his premises, and the adjoining dwellings as well. They beat Mr. Dooley up, they took him to the Quay wall just below the bridge, threw him into the river and proceeded to fire shots at him in the water, while he struggled to stay afloat. He managed to grab some branches overhanging the river and survived. Meanwhile the Auxiliaries returned to the fires and cut the hoses of the Fire Brigade. Finally the Military arrived and took charge of the situation until dawn. Naturally no one was ever charged with the murder or the arson, not that it would have made any difference even if charges had been levelled, as the R.I.C., the "Tans" and the "Auxies" had made abundantly clear to the public at large that to give evidence against any of them was to sign one's own death warrant.

Auxiliaries, demobolised officers with experience in World War I.

One further example of the ruthless behavior of this Force of "Officers and Gentlemen", who had been sent by the British Cabinet to terrorise the people of our country into subjection, was the murder of Canon Magner P.P. Dunmanway and young Tadg Crowley in December.The British Prime Minister, speaking during a cabinet debate on Dec 20th 1920, referred to the murder of Canon Magner as follows: "take the shooting of this old priest. His sole offence was to have helped a Resident Magistrate to get his motor car going and along comes a drunken beast of a soldier who makes him kneel down and shoots him". He continued by saying that he did not like the official account of the affair at all. "They were trying to say that the cadet was mad". The use of the title cadet is very misleading in the British reports of fatalities in the Auxiliaries. It implies that these battle hardened officers of the First World War (which had ended two years previously) were young recruits, which of course they were not. They were what their actions throughout the country had shown them to be from the day of their arrival, a fully trained, battle-hardened, cruel, ruthless, uncontrolled and uncontrollable force of men, not answerable to anyone except to the British Cabinet directly.

In County Cork, as well as the Black and Tans and the Auxiliaries, the people had one more cruel bunch of tormentors to contend with, the Essex Regiment of the British Armed Forces. Under the command of Col C.G. Lewes with Brevet Lt Col F.W. Moffat as Second -in-Command, this Regiment arrived at Kinsale on August 31st 1919 with a strength of 7 Officers and 201 other ranks, including band and drums.They took over

British Military Barracks, Bandon, 1920.

the personnel and equipment of the Special Reserve Battalion. The strength of the Battalion on September 1st was 40 Officers and 971 other ranks, with Companies A, B, C, and D.

- Headquarters and half of "B" Company, were stationed at Kinsale Barracks.
- Companies "C" and "D" were stationed at Queenstown, (now Cobh).
- "A" Company was stationed at Charles Fort, outside Kinsale.
- The other half of "B" Company was stationed at Bandon Military Barracks.

In 1920 Col Lewes retired and Col Moffat took over command with Major A.C. Halahan as Second-in-Command. At the end of January 1920 there were two platoons of "B" Company in Bandon. Then in March 1920, two platoons of "D" Company, under the command of the infamous Major A.E. Percival, arrived in Bandon and "B" Company was transferred to Cobh. This officer, through his conduct against the civilian population, left an indelible memory in West Cork (He was not quite so brave in World War II when, as Commander-in-Chief of British Forces in Singapore he surrendered 100,000 men to a lightly armed Japanese force of 40,000 in one of the most ignominious chapters of British history). Almost 20,000 of these British soldiers perished in Japanese Prisoner-of- War camps.

Major A.E. Percival

The history of the Essex Regiment in West Cork is indeed a tale of torture and horror. From the day of their arrival they were both arrogant and cruel and when Major Percival assumed command of this force, the die was cast for the introduction of beatings, murder and arson on a scale far greater than had hitherto been suffered by the civilian population. The following is quoted from the Essex Regimental Records:

In the Winter of 1920/21 extensive sweeps of the district were organised. During these operations practically every able-bodied civilian in the area would be searched and examined by trained intelligence officers. The dwellings of prominent partisans were also carefully marked down and many hundreds of active sympathisers were arrested and interned whilst a smaller number of really bad characters were tried and convicted of murder. But, owing to the practical disadvantages of the motor-lorry (noise), a number of badly wanted rebels escaped to the mountains of the South-west before the swoops commenced.

During these swoops, as they were transported to the area of their next round-up, part of their amusement was provided by firing at workers in the fields or bogs and innocent civilians were wounded and killed in this manner. When they captured a "rebel" they resorted to torture for their amusement.

On July 27th. 1920, Tom Hales, Brigade O.C. and Pat Harte, Brigade Quartermaster, were the recipients of Essex Regimental hospitality. Whilst on their way to meet Liam Deasy and Charlie Hurley at Hurley's of Laragh they were captured by a force of Essex. Attempts had been made to warn the Brigade Officers on their way to Hurleys of the enemy presence there but, while successful in the case of Liam Deasy and Charlie Hurley, with Hales and Harte contact could unfortunately not be made. These two brave Volunteers were captured and were taken to Bandon Military Barracks where they were recognised as Volunteers and were interrogated and tortured at length. They were punched and beaten with rifle butts, kicked, dragged up by the hair when they fell down, threatened with immediate execution whilst a revolver was pressed against their head and had all of their fingertips crushed with a pliers and their fingernails torn off. Both men survived the barbaric tortures but they had to be hospitalised. Pat Harte never recovered from the head injuries inflicted on him by the Essex "Torture Squad". It was these "gentlemen" of the British Armed Forces who also captured Volunteer John Connolly and Dick Fitzgerald as they knelt for the Rosary at Fitzgeralds of Maulnaskimlehaune on the night of September 29/30th. 1920. They too were taken to the Military Barracks and tortured. Volunteer Fitzgerald was transferred to Cork. It was sixteen days later that the mutilated body of Volunteer Connolly was found among the trees in Lord Bandon's estate where the Essex had dumped him.

Here in his own words is the story of Volunteer Frank Neville's lucky escape from death at the hands of Auxiliaries under the command of Major Percival in December 1920:

It was the 15th December 1920, twelve days after the attack at Clashanimond. All was quiet, the arms used in the attack were cleaned and dumped. I was engaged in building a gap in a fence between our place and Jagoe's farm in Raheen when suddenly there was a shout of "hands up" and three British officers jumped off the fence from the north side. One asked me my name but one of the others said "he is Neville, we know all about him and his pals Sullivan and Kelleher, we have our Intelligence working well around here now". They accused me of all the happenings in the district in which I was engaged, ambushes, the dumping and cleaning of arms in a local farmers hayshed which was correct. They had good information. I was then moved down to Jagoe's yard, to the south of where I was caught.I felt relieved because if they raided north all the (arms) dumps could have been discovered.There was a big box of explosives in a potato pit in a field quite near and a big dump full of arms and ammunition in another field not far away.

There was a big gang of Essex at Jagoe's yard. Two of them took charge and marched me away, each had the rifle muzzle in the small of my back. I was marched along the lane past Drews and Kellehers. They were all the time hurling abuse, said what a tough crowd they were, "D" Company of the Essex, and would beat the I.R.A. with their bare fists with all our buckshot and road mines. After going about a half mile, at Desmond's Lane there was another big gang of them and two or three of them commenced to beat me up.

After that I was moved along to a lane leading into Hawkes' place where the lorries were. There were two other prisoners, local men, one a Volunteer. One of the officers, Percival, they called him Major, said "put him in the last lorry he is for Cork, the other two are for Bandon". The lorries then moved away, the last one slowly, so that the others got a good way ahead. They said very little along the way. At about halfway between Tuogh Bridge and Ballinacurra there is a wood on the right with a deep glen down to the river and a hill on the other side. There was a short lane at the left leading into some fields. There the lorry stopped. I was told to get out. A soldier got out from the front of the lorry, he had a short Webley (revolver) in his hand. He pointed to the lane and said 'you get up there'. As he said that I took a step to the other side of the road. He aimed the gun at my chest and fired. I managed to tip his hand as he fired and I then bounded back along the road . He was still firing but I kept going, got across a big sheet of ice safely and got in over the fence on the right side of the road. There was another fence up and down which hid me from the soldiers. They were now out on the road. I could hear them talking and cursing. I ran up along the fence and where was a big wide gap I scrambled across it through ice and water.

A short distance from the gap there was another fence and when I got on top of that I fell over on the other side. When I tried to rise my legs were quite gone and I felt all wet along my back and chest. I thought I was wounded and opened my clothes and felt for what I thought was blood but it was only sweat. I knew then I was not hit. As my legs came to life again I made off through the brakes, there was a good cover there and it was then nearly dark. Making my way to Sullivans, Raheen, I met Pat (Sullivan) and after a while Dick Barrett, Jack Kelleher and Dan O'Mahony came. They took me to O'Mahonys, Belrose, where I collapsed from shock. After a while, having recovered, we went to Jimmy Murphys which was another safe house and I stayed there that night.

Next day I felt very shocked and was uneasy about the Raheen dumps and decided to remove all the stuff so, along with Pat Sullivan, Ned and Frank Drew we dug another big dump in a glen at Kellehers farm near the Aherla road. Another was made in an old house at Crowleys farm Belrose, but as we didn't think that a safe place, it was never used. Pat Sullivan, Ned and Frank Drew spent three or four nights removing all the stuff from Raheen to the new dumps. On Little Christmas Day (January 6th) 1921 the British made a big raid, located all the Raheen dumps but got nothing except a 'Peter the Painter' (gun) that I had in a small dump near the house at home. (Major) Percival and (Lieut.) Hotblack were in charge of these raids.

Frank Neville was indeed a lucky man. His account shows just what the Essex Regiment were capable of. It also gives us an insight into the work and the dangers of making and maintaining arms dumps, work that had to be carried out in each Company area.

Photo in British officer's album of Volunteers killed by British.

THE FORMATION OF
THE WEST CORK FLYING COLUMN

Up to July 1920 it must be understood that no agressive fighting directive had been received from Volunteer Headquarters in Dublin. The fighting areas had more or less acted on their own initiative. After the arrest of Tom Hales (on July 27th) the then Vice-Commandant of the 1st. (Bandon) Battallion Charlie Hurley, was appointed O.C. of the Brigade on August 3rd. His first priority was to organise a Brigade Flying Column.

At a Brigade Council meeting held in Coppeen, the decision to form such a column was taken. It proved to be decisive to the outcome of the War of Independence.

Early in September himself and another Brigade Officer Ted O'Sullivan, having interviewed a young ex-British army sergeant by the name of Tom Barry who had offered his services to the Bandon Volunteer Company, recommended to the Brigade Council that Barry be invited to join the Brigade as Training Officer. After further interview with Brigade Officers Liam Deasy, Sean Buckley, Dick Barrett and Charlie Hurley (in O'Mahony's house at Belrose) Barry was appointed and the first training camp was set up on the last Sunday of September 1920 at Clonbouig, Kilbrittain. This was to be an intensive training course for the officers of the eight Companies of the 1st Battallion (Bandon). More training courses followed for the officers of the Companies of the other Battalions. The personnel of the Brigade Flying Column were to be drawn in the main from the ranks. The officers in each Company were expected to the join the Flying Column whenever it was operating in their area and to participate in any ambushes or attacks carried out in that Company area.

The first mustering of the Brigade Flying Column was on October 20th at Togher. On Thursday October 24th. they engaged the enemy for the first time.This was at Toureen, three miles East of Innishannon on the Bandon-Cork road. They took up ambush positions at Robert's farm with Liam Deasy in command of the centre section of men, Charlie Hurley (Brigade O.C.) in command of the western section and Tom Barry in command of the eastern section. The ambush was a success (see "Towards Ireland Free" by Liam Deasy) and one week later on October 31st, Tom Barry was appointed Commander of the Flying Column.

From the beginning of November the Flying Column took part in almost every engagement up to the final victory over the British. Detailed accounts of all of these engagements are to be found in Liam Deasy's book "Towards Ireland Free" and Tom Barry's book "Guerilla Days in Ireland", however, there is one action to which I will refer. That is the ambush of eighteen Auxiliaries from Macroom on November 28th 1920.

The Column Commander decided to ambush them at Kilmichael, on the Macroom - Dunmanway road. Three Volunteers were killed in this ambush but the entire force of Auxiliaries was wiped out. At a British Cabinet meeting on December 1st Kilmichael ambush was referred to as a military operation with rebel forces being commanded and attacking in military formation. It was suggested that a state of siege be declared in that corner of Ireland.

By December 1920 the strength of the Third (West) Cork Brigade was 70 Companies with a total of 3,500 men. Having started the year with only 50 rifles, shotguns and a few revolvers the Brigade now had 120 rifles, shotguns, 60 revolvers and 30,000 rounds of ammunition. Although the British Forces were greater in numbers and vastly superior in armament, the morale of the Volunteers was high and the recent victories over this superior force had shown them that they could, through guerilla tactics, bring about the end of British occupation of our country.

In early December Volunteers of the 1st Cork Brigade (Cork City) attacked a group of Black and Tans at Dillon's Cross in Cork City. The reprisal that this attack evoked from the British Forces was the worst instance of arson in the entire War of Independence. On the night of December 11/12th lorry loads of heavily armed Auxiliaries left Victoria Barracks on the north side of the city and began touring Patrick Street (Cork's main thoroughfare) and adjoining streets around 6 p.m.. They harassed and abused the citizens even though curfew had not yet begun. Around 8 p.m. they began shooting indiscriminately and well before the 10 p.m. curfew they were joined by heavily armed Black and Tans and regular military.

Shortly after 10 p.m. further lorryloads of troops left the barracks with plentiful supplies of petrol in cans and drove to join their comrades on the streets. Some short time later they embarked on an undiciplined and uncontrolled orgy of arson and looting. They set fire to all the large businesses in Patrick Street. The fires spread to adjoining streets and while the Fire Brigades did their utmost to contain the fires the British Forces fired on them and cut their hoses.The City Hall because of its association with the National Cause was especially singled out for destruction as was the Carnegie Library with its thousands of books. Nor

Men of the notorious Auxiliary Division of the R.I.C.

The ruins of Cork City, December 1920.

did the R.I.C. stand aloof from the actions of the arsonists and looters. Eye witnesses saw a party of them under the control of a Head Constable turn off the water hydrants each time the firemen turned them on.

The British Labour Commission which was in Ireland at that time investigating outrages by the Crown Forces offered to produce reliable evidence to Parliament that the burning of Cork City was carried out by the Auxiliaries, Black and Tans and the Military with the collaboration of the R.I.C. but the British Government refused any enquiry into the affair.

Lieutenant-General Strickland carried out an enquiry into the affair. Lloyd George had promised Parliament, in advance, that he would publish the findings of that enquiry, but when he saw the report he did not dare to do so as it was a truly alarming document placing the blame for the burning of Cork fairly and squarely on the Crown Forces. In Parliament they blamed the I.R.A. and assured the world that the flames had spread from Patrick Street to the City Hall and to the Carnegie Library. This meant that the flames would have had to cross the River Lee which is quite wide, to reach City Hall. Sworn statements collected from English and American visitors and

General E.P. Strickland

from the citizens of Cork proved conclusively that the city had been deliberately set on fire by the forces of the Crown.

As 1920 drew to a close there was one more incident which could have seriously affected the efforts of the Volunteers. That was the excommunication decree of Dr. Cohalan, Roman Catholic Bishop of Cork, against them. Since the start of the year one Lord Mayor of Cork City had been murdered by the British in front of his family, his successor had died in Brixton Prison after 74 days on hunger-strike, martial law had been declared in Cork County and the centre of Cork City along with the City Hall and the Carnegie Library, had been burned to the ground, when Dr. Cohalan issued his decree of excommunication.

It is worth quoting here from an article by Father O'Fiach (later Cardinal O'Fiach) published in the Capuchin Annual 1970. 'The decree having been announced at the Masses in Cork on Sunday 12th December,

City Hall, Cork, 11th December 1920.

City Hall, Cork, 12th December 1920.

was published in the form of a letter to The Cork Examiner and reproduced in other newspapers on 13th December 1920. It read:

Besides the guilt involved in these acts by reason of their opposition to the Law of God, anyone who shall, within this diocese of Cork, organise or take part in an ambush or in kidnapping, or otherwise be guilty of murder or attempted murder, shall incur, by the very fact, the censure of excommunication.

J.J. Walsh T.D. (member of the Dáil) openly criticised the Bishop at a meeting of Cork Corporation for his silence on the hardships and trials of his own countrymen "not a single word of protest was uttered, and today after the city has been decimated, he saw no better course than to add insult to injury". According to Father Tomas O'Fiach this was less than fair to Dr.Cohalan.

The "London Times" newspaper lauded the Bishop's action and urged "the Hierarchy of Ireland as a whole to follow his example."

There were letters of protest against Bishop Cohalan's decree in some newspapers here at home and the "American Association for the Recognition of the Irish Republic" telegraphed its protest to the Bishop "against the use of your spiritual authority in British interests". To this the Bishop bluntly replied "nonense, I desire Irish Independence as sincerely as you. When you come up with an army able to fight the enemy and defend the weak and the unprotected, I will act as chaplain." (He obviously ignored the fact that the I.R.A. who he now excommunitated in his Diocese, was the official army of the democratically elected Government of the people of Ireland.)

On Sunday 19th December in his pastoral letter read out in every church in his Diocese he said "the killing of policemen was morally murder and politically of no consequence, and the burning of barracks was simply the destruction of Irish property.....Ordinarily there is very little risk to the ambushers themselves as there was no risk in shooting a policeman from behind a screen. Murder is murder and arson is arson whether committed by agents or by members of the Republican army and it is the duty of a Bishop to denounce murder and arson from whatever source they come." (Capuchin Annual 1970).

But the reaction of the Volunteers to the decree could have seriously affected the outcome of the fight for freedom as the Volunteers were in the main deeply religous men who obeyed their bishops in matters of faith and religion. Likewise the women of Cumann na mBan and all who were helping the Volunteers were profoundly troubled by the decree.

Many of the Volunteers believed that Bishop Cohalan was wrong and continued the fight. Some of the priests continued to administer the Sacraments to them and some of the priests made no secret of the fact that they thought their Bishop was wrong.(see "Guerilla Days in Ireland" by Tom Barry)

The patriot priest Father Dominic O.F.M.Cap. in a letter sent on the day of his arrest to Florrie O'Donoghue, Adjutant Cork No. 2 Brigade, with reference to the Bishop's decree made distinctions between kidnapping, ambushing and killing carried out by private persons which "would fall under the excommunication" and such acts carried out "by and with the authority of the State, the Republic of Ireland, and the State has the right and duty to defend the lives and property of its citizens and to punish, even with death, those who are aiming at the destruction of lives or property of its citizens or itself." The letter then goes on to deal with the attitude to be adopted towards the excommunication in practice, "there is no need to worry about it. Let the boys keep going to Mass and Confession and Communion as usual".

Because of Father Dominic the crisis of concience was averted and the fight continued with by now, the full backing of the people.

1920 had been a decisive year. The Black and Tans, the Auxiliaries and the Essex Regiment by their actions in the Cork area, drove more and more people into opposition against Dublin Castle (the seat of British rule in Ireland) and the British Government and made them more sympathtetic towards the Volunteers. Many of the old R.I.C did not take too kindly to their new,and better paid Auxiliary colleagues, or to their methods, and resigned in large numbers in 1920.

BANDON TOWN

In Bandon town the number of active Volunteers numbered only twelve. One must take cognisance of the fact that, within the town itself there was a population of at least 3,000 people, many of whom would have been strong Loyalists. There were also at least 300 British ex-service men in the town, not long back from the World War and while some of them (like Tom Barry) joined the Volunteers, most of them looked askance at the efforts to throw off the English yoke. The atmosphere in the town was not congenial to the activities of the Volunteers. They were viewed by the business community as a de-stabilising influence on the cosy "status quo" that was guaranteed by the presence of British Forces garrisoned in the town. The Volunteers were up against it all the time but they were certainly there. At this point it is probably appropriate to re-emphasise that only a small minority of the Irish population took an active or even a semi-active part in the fight for Independence. The people of West Cork who gave food, shelter and first aid to the Volunteers "on the run", were not the the proprietors of large businesses nor the wealthy home owners but those from homes that were austere enough already, the small farmers, teachers, labourers, shop assistants, railway workers, office workers etc. and it was from the same background that most of the Volunteers themselves came.

The number of fulltime active members in Bandon was so small that the amount of work to be done was enormous. For instance, in addition to other duties, you had the collection of the Arms Fund in the town performed by members of the Company and seizures had to be made from defaulters. It frequently happened that the enemy troops would make a swoop on a street when the men of the Company would be engaged in making collections and would close both ends of the street in an effort to capture those engaged in this task. Often the men had a narrow escape.

A number of citizens of the town were compelled by the British to report daily to the Military Barracks and to the R.I.C. Barracks as a cover for the British Forces own local informants who were habitually

Dr. Dorothy Stopford, protestant lady doctor who at great personal risk treated many volunteers

calling to the Barracks. This necessitated the posting of men from the local Company to a house overlooking the entrances to both Barracks for the observation of such callers and a daily report had to be made to Battalion Headquarters. This very important duty continued right up to the Truce. The men of the Company who were detailed to remain in the town for this activity were men who had special knowledge of covering positions and lines of retreat and they were utilised as guides and scouts by the Column and members of the Battalion and Brigade Staffs when any of them were about to enter, or leave, the town.

Three members of the Company were detailed for the daily handling of dispatches and the transmission of same to Battalion Headquarters at Skeaf, to Brigade Headquarters (where located) and to adjoining Companies . They also had to deal with intercepted Police and Military messages from 1919 up to the Truce and the speedy transmission of same to "Key" houses in the town or suburbs. From August 1919 it had been arranged that all Military and Police messages, outgoing or incoming to Bandon Post Office, were deciphered and rushed out immediately to Brigade Headquarters. As Brigade H.Q. was not at any time located on the South side of the Bandon River before the Truce, the men taking out dispatches to the Farnivane Company, for onward transmission, had to pass through the 100 yards separating the Military Barracks on the Square, and the Black and Tan Barracks on Kilbrogan Hill. (There was another Barracks on the South side of the town, occupied by the R.I.C. and for a time, by the Black and Tans).

Because of the curfew mentioned heretofore the men of the Company in the performance of their duties had to slip in and out of the town between Military and Police patrols. The town and its immediate surroundings were fraught with danger for the Volunteers.

Early in the month of December 1920, the then Company Captain, John Galvin, and two other Volunteers from the Bandon Company Jim O'Donoghue and Joe Begley, were going to meet with Tom Barry when they were ambushed on the outskirts of the town, and were captured. They were beaten tortured and then shot through the forehead by Enemy troops who were "lying in", a new procedure adopted by the Enemy on the off chance of intercepting members of the Volunteers outward bound with dispatches or guns etc, or incoming as the case may be. Many others of the Company had narrow escapes because of the adoption of this method of "lying in" by the Enemy.

*The remains of Volunteers, Begley, Galvin and O'Donoghue
who were tortured and shot outside Bandon in December 1920.*

A number of men were detailed to watch for the movement of enemy columns stationed in the town and had immediately on noting the movement of a column out of the town, to shadow that column and report in advance to the Company area to which that column was heading, and to warn of it's approach. In this way every move that the enemy column made was known in advance throughout the Battalion area and the Volunteers were at their sharpest. This was a fulltime duty for the men concerned and necessitated great patience. Another duty which was very important to the Brigade at this time, and later of paramount importance to the Flying Column, was that of the boatmen at Shippool and Kilmacsimon who ferried the Brigade officers and men across the River Bandon and the men who scouted for them at Innishannon bridge, Baxter's Bridge and other crossings on the Bandon River throughout the War of Independence. All of these brave men and women served our country well, and though to many their task might appear to have been without much danger, they risked capture, torture and death each time that they ferried their comrades across the river. They shared the same danger of reprisals against themselves and their families as any who helped the men "on the run" did. Many of them sometimes found their duties boring and would have preffered to be in action against the enemy but, it was essential that they be there at the river crossings when required. Their's was a vital contribution to the War of Independence.

John "Flyer" Nyhan (standing left), Jim "Spud" Murphy (standing right), and Mick Crowley (seated).

1921 THE YEAR OF FINAL VICTORY

The British Labour Party had commissioned a report on the situation in Ireland in 1920 and the conclusion arrived at in this report (which was published in January 1921), was that "things are being done in the name of Britain which would make our name stink in the nostrils of the whole world."

In December 1920 the British put out some peace feelers. In the House of Commons on December 10th Hamar Greenwood offered a truce if the rebels laid down their arms and surrendered their extremist leaders. Lloyd George tried to communicate with Sinn Fein through Archbishop Patrick Joseph Clune, the Roman Catholic Archbishop of Perth, Australia who was in England at that time. He was instructed to meet with Sinn Fein leaders and see if a truce might be possible. The conditions laid down by the British for a Truce were:

1. All arms, ammunition, uniforms and explosives in the area under martial law were to be surrendered to the Government.
2. All arms in the rest of Ireland to be handed over to the safe custody of the Government and no distinction to be made between the rest of Ireland and Ulster.
3. Sinn Fein to order the cessation of all violence in return for which the Government would stop reprisals, shop looting, raids, burnings, floggings, execution without courtmartial (not admitted) and people only to be executed after due courtmartial.
4. Sinn Fein M.P.s (except a specific list) to be allowed to assemble. ("Whitehall Diary", Thomas Jones. Oxford University Press.).

The attitude of the Volunteers to the approach made through Archbishop Clune was very sceptical. The conditions laid down by the British Government were treated with derision. The successes of 1920 by a small guerilla army against vastly superior highly trained and well armed forces had given the Volunteers the confidence to bring about the final victory.

By the end of December 1920 the incidence of murder, arson, beatings and the humilation of the civilian population had increased more and more. Martial Law was extended to Counties Clare, Wexford, Waterford and Kilkenny on January 6th 1921. General Strickland C.O. of the Cork area ordered that a list be placed behind the front door of every house giving the name, age and occupation of each inhabitant. When a house was raided everyone on that list had to be accounted for.

During this month General Macready sanctioned the blowing up of houses belonging to members of the I.R.A. by the Army (this only gave offical sanction to what the Black and Tans and the Auxiliaries had been doing since 1919). At this time also the death penalty was introduced for helping or harbouring the Volunteers. Macready assured the British Cabinet that in another three months he would have the I.R.A. crushed as they were according to him, already demoralised and tired of the fight and were surrendering their arms. He also assured them that the forces of the Crown had at last definitely gained the upper hand. A final sustained onslaught against the I.R.A. by the forces under his command would ensure victory and the return of peace in Ireland.

What Macready did not know was that Lloyd George already viewed Ireland as lost to the Empire.

Tom Hales, first Commandant
of the Brigade.

Seán Buckley, Brigade I/O and
member of the Brigade Staff.

SETBACKS

1921

From the beginning of the year the I.R.A. went on the offensive against the occupation forces. They attempted to ambush the police and the military at every opportunity. The enemy would no longer dare to venture out of their barracks except in large numbers, usually in sorties of not less than three or four lorryloads. It was their practice also to carry either a captured Volunteer or a civilian on board the lorries to guard against ambush. In the West Cork Brigade area although the Brigade Flying Column tried to ambush them again and again throughout the month of January, only four attempts were successful and none of the four was decisive.

In February the West Cork Brigade suffered a number of serious setbacks.

At the beginning of February a planned attack on the R.I.C. Barracks at Rosscarbery was aborted when a postman reported the presence of the Column at Burgatia House (about a mile from the vilage) to the police and they with a strong force of Black and Tans attempted to surround Burgatia House. The fight that ensued is very well recorded in Liam Deasy's book "Towards Ireland Free". It is sufficient here to state that the Column escaped the trap.

On February 4th Lieutenant Paddy Crowley, a very able leader in the Kilbrittain Company, was shot dead while trying to fight his way out of an enemy roundup at Ardacrow. An attack on Drimoleague R.I.C. Barracks on the night of February 11th. was unsuccessful when the mine used failed to breach the wall of the barracks. On the 16th of the month an ambush of the Cork-Bandon train on which twelve or fifteen soldiers were reported to be travelling from Cork, was carried out at Upton Station. News of fifty soldiers from Kinsale joining the train at Kinsale Junction did not reach the Volunteers at Upton and the ambush was a disaster. The Flying Column had seven casualties out of the fourteen men in the ambush party, three dead and four including the Brigade O.C., wounded. One Volunteer was captured. This was the most serious reverse experienced to date by the West Cork Brigade. It was quickly followed by another. Volunteers from the Kilbrittain Company were trenching the road at Croisnaleanbh Cross Roads when they were surprised by an enemy patrol. Four of the Volunteers were killed that night. In the first sixteen days of February eight volunteers of the Brigade had paid the supreme sacrifice for Ireland. All of these encounters are recorded in Liam Deasy's and in Tom Barry's books and make enthralling reading of betrayal and courage.

Nor had the adjoining Brigade areas escaped the increased activity of the Crown Forces during January and February. At Dripsey in the Cork Number One Brigade area, the Donoghmore Company was surprised and five Volunteers were captured. Four of them were executed and the fifth died of his wounds in prison. At the Battle of Clonmult also in that Brigade area on February 20th, the entire column of the Midleton Battalion was almost wiped out. Five of the Volunteers were killed in the fight. Seven were shot after they had surrendered and two others were summarily executed. In another engagement at Mourneabbey in the Cork Number Two Brigade area, five volunteers of the Mallow Battalion column were killed and two who were captured were executed later.

Although February 1921 had in many ways been a disastrous month in the three Cork Brigade areas the fight had been taken to the enemy at all times and despite the loss of so many experienced comrades the morale of the Volunteers was still high. Their constant attacks had succeeded in forcing the enemy to travel only in large numbers, which travel was made more and more difficult because of the increased road trenching in all Company areas. They had also forced them to abandon many of their barracks throughout County Cork thus the R.I.C. (the eyes and ears of the British Authorities) were removed from large areas of the County.

It is noteworthy that by the end of February General Macready had re-assessed his emphatic declaration to Lloyd George at the start of the year regarding his inevitable victory over the I.R.A.. In December Hamar Greenwood had said that victory would be in two months, General Tudor had said three months and General Macready had said four months. Now, three months on, while insisting that the I.R.A. would be crushed he refused to put a date on it.

On February 22nd the Flying Column had a successful encounter with the enemy in 'Bandon. In this action three Black and Tans and two soldiers were killed while the men of the Column were unharmed. Later on that night Tom Barry decided to stand down the Column until March 12th. The men had been marching, lying in ambush and harassing the Crown Forces on a continuous basis since the beginning of the year and needed a well earned rest.

Liam Deasy and Tom Barry now directed their attention to a proposed ambush of soldiers of the Essex Regiment stationed at Kinsale. A large force of these troops travelled from Kinsale to Bandon and back on a regular basis.

On Sunday March 13th accompanied by a scouting party from the Innishannon Company (T. Butler, T. Cummins, D. Buckley, M. Crowley, J. Finn and D. Finn) they proceeded to the Bandon - Kinsale Road to survey the area and to select the positions best suited for the ambush. The site chosen was directly opposite the old castle of Dun-na-Long at Shippool. The day chosen for the ambush was Thursday the 17th of March, St. Patrick's Day. That night they joined the Column which was now mobilised at Behagh. The plan was that the Column would set out from Behagh on the Monday night and march in stages to the ambush site at Shippool, a distance of some thirty miles. The intention was that they would arrive there before dawn on Thursday. There would be two stops on the march, the first at Lissnagat, the second at Rearour.

On the evening of Wednesday, 16th March 1921, while Charlie Hurley the Brigade O/C and Flor Begley Brigade Acting Adj., were at Brigade headquarters (which was in the house of Humphrey and Denis Forde, Ballymurphy, Upton), Charlie informed Flor that the Brigade Flying Column was at Tough (or Rearour) and suggested that they would both go over to see the lads. Flor told him that he had about an hours work to do and said he would follow Charlie over to O'Mahony's of Belrose, (a regular safe house in the Knockavilla or Crosspound Company area - both being one and the same Company) and from there they would proceed to meet the lads of the Column.

They met at O'Mahony's about an hour later, as arranged, and as they walked towards Tom Kelleher's of Crow Hill they met Liam Deasy (then Brigade Adjutant) Tom Barry (Flying Column O.C.), Tadg Sullivan (Brigade Quartermaster) Denis Lordan and Mick Crowley. Denis was the Flying Column Adjutant and Mick was the Brigade Engineer.

After handshakes all round and a short chat in the boreen, Liam Deasy asked Flor Begley (also the Brigade Piper) if he had his bagpipes at headquarters and if he would accompany the Column the following day, Thursday, St. Patrick's Day, as it was intended to celebrate it in style by ambushing some lorries to the accompaniment of the warpipes. Liam then made arrangements to have the pipes collected and brought to O'Mahony's, later that evening. They all then proceeded from the boreen

O'Mahony's family home, Belrose House, later burned by British forces.

to O'Mahony's house. On the way they called into Crosspound public house, where they remained only a few minutes.

They stayed at O'Mahony's house for a few hours and had their tea there. Later Dick Barrett, Sean Buckley and Tom Kelleher arrived. They sat around and discussed the recent ambush at Upton, current happenings and plans for future campaigns. At around midnight the others rose to leave the house and Charlie said "Flor we had better be going home too" (they looked on Headquarters as being home, and no wonder they as Fordes, Ballymurphy, had been Brigade Headquarters for many months prior to that evening).

Tom Barry almost immediately said "Flor is coming with us Charlie". "What?", said Charlie, "For the skirl of the pipes and the crack of the rifles, I am coming too". Liam Deasy and Tom Barry persuaded him not to attempt to come. They felt that he was not physically fit as a result of his wounds and sprained ankle incurred during the Upton Train ambush some five weeks earlier. It was impressed upon him, that if the column had a long retreat after the proposed ambush at Shippool the next day he could not possibly stand up to it. He was bitterly disappointed. Flor Begley had been his constant companion for many months and now he saw himself as an invalid unable to accompany his comrades on the planned ambush. In his disappointment he said "Well Flor, let me hear the pipes before you go, play a few tunes for me". The piper did, and that was the last time those two great comrades saw each other.

That night (Wednesday March 16th 1921) Liam Deasy, Tom Barry, Tadg O'Sullivan, Flor Begley and Tom Kelleher joined the Flying Column at Rearour. The column then proceeded to Shippool, on the Bandon - Kinsale road, arriving there in the early hours of Thursday morning (St. Patrick's Day). The Innishannon Company had been mobilised that night at Coolmoreen and met the Column at Slievegullane and scouted it to Shippool as dawn was breaking. The Column immediately took up ambush positions. There were one hundred and two volunteers including four Brigade Officers at Shippool on that morning, the largest the Flying Column had ever been since its formation in November 1920.

All that day the column lay in wait for the convoy of Essex soldiers who normally travelled that road every day. It was a cold miserable wait, during which the volunteers had only the tea and bread supplied by the Hurley and O'Leary families nearby to sustain them. That day the Essex did not travel and at dusk that evening the Column, drenched and frozen to the bone, returned to the townland of Skeough which is situated between the Bandon - Cork road and the Innishannon - Kinsale road. Here the Column billeted that Thursday night and all day Friday in the warm hospitality and generous atmosphere of the homes of the people there. With the Innishannon Company on Guard, the column, though disappointed, could rest and relax and they celebrated St. Patrick's night in safety.

The following morning, at O'Leary's Slievegullane, Liam Deasy, Tom Barry, Tadg O'Sullivan and Dr. Con Lucey (Brigade medical Officer) decided that the Column should move to Crossbarry and hopefully would engage a column of British troops passing on the north Bandon to Cork road.

Tom Kelleher, Captain of the Ballyhandle Company, had expert local knowledge of the terrain at Crossbarry and having consulted with Brigade O/C and the Column O/C he was instructed to proceed to the area and organise food and billets for the men of the Column. It was also the duty of the local volunteer Company to provide guards and scouts for the overnight security of the Column. If attacked the Column were responsible for their own defence. The risks run by the owners of the houses in which the men were billeted were very real and very great, often resulting in the burning of their houses and in either prison or death for the owners if discovered by the British forces.

CROSSBARRY, THE DECISIVE BATTLE

The Brigade Column left Slievegullane at dusk on the night of 18th. March 1921 and arrived at Pat O'Leary's, Ballyhandle at about 1 a.m. and his house became Column H.Q. An immediate evaluation of the proposed ambush position (west of the village) was undertaken by the Column O/C (Tom Barry) and the Brigade Adjutant (Liam Deasy) and the H.Q. post and position of each section was decided. The sections were sent to their pre-arranged billets with final instructions to all sections to parade at 6 a.m. and, in the event of an alarm before 6 a.m, to parade at O'Learys. Even in the darkness it was agreed that the position was not a good one. That part in the area of Harold and Beasleys was very good but the rising ground behind the fences and the shallow fence cover from there to Crossbarry bridge was not only unsuitable, but also dangerous to retire from under fire.

On their way back to O'Leary's, Tom Barry and Liam Deasy met Dan Canty and John Lordan of Newcestown and they retired to Cronin's public house for a drink before going to their billets. At O'Leary's, Barry and Deasy were joined by Tadg O'Sullivan (the Column Quartermaster) and after a few exchanges on plans they all retired for a sleep. The time was approximately 12.30 a.m. It was now the morning of one of the most historic battles in the history of Ireland's 700 year struggle for freedom against British forces. This battle proved to be the final great battle in the long struggle.

While the column members slept, the volunteers of the local Company, captained by Tom Kelleher, kept watch in the area. At 2.30 a.m. Tom Kelleher and Mick Crowley rushed in to O'Leary's to report that scouts outside the western end of the area reported seeing the lights of, and hearing the noise of, lorries approaching some miles away from the directon of Bandon. This was the beginning of the encirclement of the area by British forces which resulted from information given by a captured volunteer to British Army Intelligence officers in Cork jail, and which, later that morning, resulted in the capture of Brigade Headquarters at Fordes of Ballymurphy and the subsequent death of Charlie Hurley, Brigade O/C.

Sean Mac Carthy's letter to Liam Deasy 18.7.63:

In haste,

Liam a cara,

You are quite right about the eve of Toureen. Dick Barrett supported Charlie's attitude by adding "that it was not possible to arm those volunteers already available".

Did you ever hear of the eve of Crossbarry? I was going along Patrick Street in Cork when Fr. Ned Fitzgerald (now Canon in Ballinlough), son of Sir Edward (Fitzy) approached me and said "Senior officers in Cork Barrack were seen going with maps into ....'s cell today and it bodes no good, I think the boys should be told".

I dashed off home by the evening train, and went off up to Belrose Hs. where I met Charlie, Sean Buckley and Dick Barrett. Charlie had a lame leg having jumped off the railway bridge during the Upton ambush. He had O'Connell's or Forde's tub trap and pony and Sean Buckley was with him. I told Fr. Ned's Story and appealed to them, as Sean Buckley can tell you, "to clear away west".

At 12.30 I went with them to the end of the avenue again beseeching them, but Chariey remarked "we have the pony and we will chance it tonight anyway". He was shot early the following morning. Sean B. was in another house and got away as a local carpenter, to be searched for later all over the place. Dick Barrett said T. Barry's Column was along the Kinsale railway and no one knew what he would do. I should clear back to Cork early.

Sean Mac.

Sean Buckley had beseeched Charlie to go with him to O'Connell's farm in Ballinphellig (across the bog from Forde's in Ballymurphy,). Charlie's response was that Denis Forde (in whose home Charlie had been living for some months now), would remain up all night to put the pony away as he expected Charlie to return.

As stated earlier the British had captured a Volunteer at the ambush at Upton Station on February 16th and taken him to Cork Jail. He was courtmartialed on a charge of waging war on Crown Forces. Sentence was never promulgated and he was only interned in Castletownbere from where he was released with other internees in December 1921. While being held under sentence of death at Cork Jail he asked to see the Military Intelligence Officers at the jail. To save his own life he told them that Brigade Headquarters was in the Ballymurphy townland area, though he did not know in which house it was in. He gave them quite a lot of other information as well.

As a result of the information they had received from the captured Volunteer the British military now knew Brigade H.Q. was in the Ballymurphy area. Immediately they set about planning its encirclement and destruction with the capture of all volunteer personnel there and the huge quantities (as they thought) of arms and ammunition that they were certain would be there. Throughout the War of Independence, they never knew the number of volunteers that they were up against (or the arms they carried), but by late 1920 they grossly overestimated the strength of the Irish Republican Army.

The British formulated a plan to surround the Ballymurphy townland area using troops from Bandon, Cork, Ballincollig, Kinsale and Macroom. According to British records the troops were to be transported to within four miles of the area to be encircled at which point half of the troops were to dismount and proceed on foot in line abreast towards Ballymurphy townland. They were to raid every house in the area and to arrest all adult males. The soldiers on foot were to interchange periodically with those remaining on the lorries, thus ensuring fresh troops throughout the operation.

The encirclement began about 1 a.m. on the morning of March 19th 1921. The British troops were the cream of British military forces in Ireland at that time, many of them having seen action in the World War of 1914-1918. They were drawn from the Hampshire Regiment (stationed in Cork) the Essex Regiment (stationed in Bandon and Kinsale and the infamous Auxiliaries (all ex World War officers) stationed in Macroom. Each group was alloted a specific number of farms to be surrounded and searched.

While the column did not know of the planned encirclement of the Ballymurphy area, neither did the British know of the presence of one hundred and four men of the Flying Column (the strongest it had ever been), in the area.

1st Action

Some time after 7 a.m. the Brigade Adj. (L. Deasy) and the Column O.C. (Tom Barry) took up positions at Denis Lordans Section E opposite where one mine was laid (with Peter Monahan in charge). It was planned that sections A,B,C, & D would not fire at the five or six lorries as they passed so that the entire convoy of troops would be inside the trap. Hence the importance of E Section and the reason for the Column Commander's presence there. Should the convoy come from Cork then they would have been allowed to pass from the east in front of sections E,D,C & B to Harolds Old Lane where a second mine had been laid with Dan Holland in charge.

It is interesting to note here that the troops missed out on the capture of the Brigade Intelligence Officer, Sean Buckley, during this round-up. On that morning, he was taken prisoner at the outside farm of Mrs. O'Connell of Ballymurphy. This farm was located at Ballinphellig, and Sean was arrested with Tim O'Connell (son of the owner) and a workman named Roche when the farm was raided by the Hampshire Regiment.

Miss J. Forde, a step sister of O'Connell pleaded with the officer in charge of the raiding party not to take all the men saying "could he, the Major, not leave her some one of them to milk the cows?". He eventually left the three of them, but he emphasised that he would be back to check on them within an hour and warned them not to attempt to leave as there were "three hundred of our men" in the area and "if you attempt to leave you will be caught".

Sean Buckley had been extremely fortunate that it was members of the Hampshire Regiment that had conducted this raid as they failed to recognise him. Had they been members of the Essex Regiment from Bandon to whom the Brigade Intelligence Officer was well known, and by whom he had been continually sought, they would have made a very important capture indeed.

Shortly after the raiding party left the house and yard, firing was heard across the bog at Ballymurphy. Thus began the next action of that historical morning.

2nd Action
The time was now 7 a.m. and another raiding party, led by a Major Hallinan approached the farmhouse of Denis Forde, which was now, and had been for some months, the Brigade H.Q. Inside with the family was Charlie Hurley, the Brigade O.C.. When the Major banged at the door demanding entry, Charlie rushed down the stairs and fired through the door, wounding Major Hallinan (see note re steel jacket) and then attempted to make his escape through the back door. Just as he got outside the door, he was shot through the head by a soldier running to cover the rear of the house. The soldier had shot from the hip whilst running and by a fluke had hit Charlie in the head.

Thus it was that the young life of a great man was brought to an untimely end. It is ironic that Charlie had no idea that the Flying Column were just down the road at Crossbarry. There can be no doubt, that had he known, wounded or not, he would have joined them the night before and would have been in the thick of the battle that morning. His body was taken to the military barracks in Bandon and was seen there by Dr. Welply who was medical officer to the military there.

Some three weeks previously Flor Begley had arranged to meet Dr. Welply at Crossbarry and had accompanied him in his car to Barters of Ballinphellig (the agreed rendevous) to attend to Charlie because the wounds he had received at Upton ambush were not healing well (not in Fordes as this was their H.Q.). Now some three weeeks later at Bandon military barracks, whilst attending the British dead and wounded, Dr. Welply saw the bodies of the four volunteers taken from Crossbarry to Bandon and did not recognise Charlie Hurley. He told Flor Begley that he had examined a large bruise on the chest of Major Hallinan who told him that he would have been killed by the shots through the door had he not being wearing a steel plate inside his uniform.

The shots that Charlie Hurley fired, and those that killed him, were the first shots of the Crossbarry Battle.

3rd Action

Crossbarry was planned to be the ambush of five or six lorries of troops known to travel the back road from Bandon to Cork via Crossbarry. The fight that materialised was neither planned or expected by the I.R.A. or the British forces. It was the largest and most important battle of the opposing forces in West Cork, resulting in an historic victory for the I.R.A. and a demoralising defeat for the cream of the British occupation forces. Each member of the Flying Column had only 40 rounds of ammunition when the battle commenced.

The alarm having been raised at 2.30 a.m.(when the lorries of troops had been seen and heard by the sentries) all sections were alerted and the Column was on parade at O'Leary's, as arranged, before 3 a.m. They then moved to the field behind Beasley's house at the western end of the ambush positions. The engineering party, accompanied by a protection unit, then moved off towards Crossbarry bridge at the eastern end of the ambush positions where they proceeded to dig a hole in the road and placed a mine there. Peter "Scottie" Monahan was in charge of detonating this mine. A second mine was planted near Harolds Lane at the western end of the ambush area and this was under the charge of Dan Holland.

The rest of the Column waited from 3 a.m. to 6 a.m. in the field behind Beasleys. This long wait for further news of what was happening since the lorries were first seen coming from the direction of Bandon was spent huddled against the fences without food or sleep, the men having had only one hours sleep before the alarm was raised at 2.30 a.m. It was a dry but bitterly cold night.

By dawn the volunteers had moved into their appointed sections as chosen by the Column O.C., the Brigade Adj. and Denis Lordan on their arrival at Crossbarry the previous night.

There were seven sections and, as can be seen from the accompanying fold-out map at the back of the book, they stretched from Harolds Lane at the western end to the bend of the road before Crossbarry village at the eastern end of the chosen ambush position.

The Section Commanders were:

Section "A": Sean Hales
Section "B": John Lordan
Section "C": Mick Crowley   **SEE FOLD-OUT MAP**
Section "D": Pete Kearney   **AT BACK OF BOOK**
Section "E": Denis Lordan
Section "F": Tom Kelleher
Section "G": Christy O'Connell

The sections were now inspected by the Column O.C.Tom Barry and at 7 a.m. every section was in readiness with Tom Kelleher's section and Christy O'Connell's section protecting the Column's rear and flanks.

The flying Column was organised into sections of 14 men as against the usual army sections of between 7 and 10 men. The reason for this was due to a number of factors.

The Column, almost constantly on the move, had to make its own arrangements for its protection day and night. Scouts and sentries were provided by local companies, but the Column's defence fell on the men of the Column. Because of this a smaller section would not be adequate to stem a frontal, rear or flanking attack, nor could the Column Commander afford to divert two or more smaller sections to the left or right flanks or to the rear in the event of an attack.

There was an obvious advantage in having only one section commander responsible for rear or flank positons. The organisation of the Column into sections of 14 men was dictated by the conditions prevailing at that time in West Cork.

82

As the battle progressed the efficiency of the Section Commanders becomes apparent and the morale engendered by the belief of the volunteers in their section commanders and the Brigade O.C. and Column O.C., coupled with their own fierce determination and bravery shown against vastly superior forces attempting to surround the area, brought about the historic victory that was Crossbarry.

When the section positions for the planned ambush of the five or six lorries expected to be normally travelling from Bandon to Cork on that road, were chosen by the Column O.C. and the Brigade Adj, it was envisiged that sections A,B,C & D would allow the lorries to pass until the leading lorry was over the mine opposite Denis Lordans Section ("E") at which point Peter "Scottie" Monahan would detonate the mine and all the troops would be in the trap. Should the lorries come from the east (from Cork) then they would not be fired on by sections E,D,C, or B until the leading lorry was over the mine at Harold's Lane, this then to be detonated by Dan Holland.

Dan Holland

At this point in time, the Column, which was now at its greatest strength ever, (one hundred and four officers and men and fourteen local scouts) had no awareness of the planned encirclement of the Ballymurphy townland area or the hundreds of troops involved. Neither did the enemy have any knowledge that the West Cork Flying Column, so long a huge thorn in their side and from whom they were still smarting after their defeat at Kilmichael some four months before, was in the area.

Now circumstances had changed for the Flying Column and though they did not know it, the planned ambush of five or six lorries, was to become a battle for their very survival and finally a huge demoralising defeat for the cream of the Crown forces in Ireland.

Two unarmed scouts, Tadg O'Sullivan and Desmond were sent to bring Charlie Hurley in from H.Q. but were captured in the round up.

4th Action
Scouts had earlier reported the sound of lorries approaching slowly from the west. This slow movement of the lorries (first sighted at 2.30 a.m.) puzzled the leaders. The Column was in position and waiting.

Everything was in readiness for the planned ambush of five or six lorries but the Battle of Crossbarry which was about to begin, would involve far greater numbers of ememy forces than this contingent. Sometime after 7 a.m. Liam Deasy and Tom Barry took up position at Section E (Lordan's) already chosen as ambush H.Q.

Then, shortly after 7 a.m., the quiet of that calm sunny March morning was shattered by the sound of gunfire from the north east. This was the first indication the column had of any enemy activity other than in the west from where the first lorries were reported. Reports from other scouts indicated activity throughout the entire area and it became obvious to the

Tadg O'Sullivan,
Brigade Quartermaster.

Brigade Adj and the Column O.C. that major activity by the enemy was in progress. On re-appraising the situation it appeared that the attack might now have to be a breakout from what seemed to be an encircling movement.

The shots first heard came from the direction of Denis Fordes house (about one and a half miles north east of the ambush position) and it was clear that the Brigade O.C. Charlie Hurley who was recuperating at Fordes, was now under attack. Liam Deasy and Tom Barry immediately determined to go to his rescue. It was decided that Liam should take sections "A","B","C", and that Tom would take sections "D","E", and "F" and proceed independently to the high ground above O'Briens quarry at Ballyhandle, on the Crossbarry-Begleys Forge road, there to meet and review the situation again.

Liam Deasy left Denis Lordan's section ("E") and had barely gone 15 yards in the direction of the western sections when he heard lorries approaching those sections. He shouted back to the Column Commander "Do you hear that noise?" but his words were lost in the bursts of rifle fire and the skirl of bagpipes that now came from the direction of Harolds and Beasleys at the western end of the ambush positions.

The Battle of Crossbarry had begun.

5th Action

The ambush did not proceed as originally planned. All sections were under strict orders to remain out of sight of the enemy until all of the five or six lorries expected were within the 600 yard ambush position. However, when only three of the lorries had entered the trap, one volunteer perhaps through over-anxiety, poked his rifle out of an upper window in Beasleys barn and this action was seen by the driver of the first lorry. He immediately brought his lorry to a stop and shouted his warning.

John Lordan, commander of "B" section realised what had happened and ordered his volunteers to open fire on the enemy. Hales' men in "A" section and Mick Crowley's men in "C" section immediately opened fire as well. None of the lorries were full of soldiers as they approached the ambush site. There were about eight or ten men in each. Some of the complement of each lorry had been moving forward on foot, in tandem with the lorries, as part of the round up.

The volunteers in "G" section, under the command of Christy O'Connell opened fire on those lorries which had not yet entered the ambush position and also came into contact with the enemy on foot, moving in from the western end and attempting to outflank the column.

As the fight raged in front of sections "A", "B" and "C" the enemy fought bravely, but finally broke and the survivors ran towards the railway embankment south of the road. They were joined by some of the soldiers from the other lorries and some on foot. Peter Kearney and Denis Lordan, whose sections ("D"&"E") were not yet engaged in the fighting, nor likely to be engaged as they were further east along the road, saw that the enemy intended to gain the cover of the railway embankment to the south and immediately led their men across the road to cut off this enemy move. They were joined in this by Liam Deasy and Tom Barry both of whom had already left Denis Lordan's section and were rushing to sections "A","B"& "C". After about 15 minutes fighting they succeeded in thwarting any ideas the enemy had of taking up positions on the embankment, or of moving into positions closer to Beasleys. When the action was over those soldiers who had not been either killed or wounded, had escaped over the embankment and these were still running south when Peter Kearney, Denis Lordan and their men returned to their original positions. Liam Deasy now went to Mick Crowleys section "C" and Tom Barry went to section "B" where fighting was still going on.

The three lorries that had entered the ambush site were quite close together and the volunteers in sections "A", "B", and "C" were very fortunate that early in the fight a bullet had penetrated the drum of a machine gun mounted on one of the lorries, thereby jamming the gun. Later, a Volunteer, Edward White, who was a prisoner on one lorry (having been captured earlier that morning at Kilpatrick while carrying a dispatch) and who jumped from the lorry during the ambush, carried the captured Lewis gun during the column's withdrawal. Also during the engagement a bomb was thrown by the British soldiers and landed inside the ditch, Paddy o'Sullivan, Cromhane (Beara) went forward and threw it back on to the road where it exploded.

Harolds' farmyard where Flor Begley marched during the fighting.

At the start of the fighting Flor Begley, the Brigade piper, proceeded to play martial airs on his warpipes which, at the behest of Liam Deasy, Brigade Adjutant, he had brought along to celebrate St.Patricks Day,. He continued to play while the firing lasted. Among the tunes he played on that fateful day were "Let Erin Remember", "Eamonn a Chnuic" and "Wrap the Green Flag round me Boys".Certain theorists have since declared that he would have been better off with a rifle in his hands that morning but they have not got all the wisdon of the world or knowledge of that day. Volunteers who fought at Crossbarry, spoke later of the way the piper caused the blood to course through their veins, and the way the warpipes awakened the ferocity in their hearts that made them truly dangerous to their enemies. Tom Kelleher often said over the years that followed, "that man's music was more effective than twenty rifles" on that morning.

The piper also had an effect on the morale of the British troops. They would have associated a piper with a battalion in their army, and consequently would have thought that there were many more volunteers present than there really were. Liam Deasy, writing some forty years later, says in his book "Towards Ireland Free" that "this was Begleys finest hour and one on account of which he will be ever remembered as "The Piper Of Crossbarry". It is of interest to note that a pipe Sgt.Major of an Irish Battalion in the Lebanon recently, was decorated for similar actions during an engagement there.

6th Action

As Liam Deasy met Mick Crowley in "C" section, firing was still going on in sections "A" and "B". Suddenly came the sound of firing from a new and unexpected point, rather close, from their immediate rear or rear left flank. Crowley and himself concluded that it was Tom Kelleher's section "F" in action, and it was realised for the first time that there was movement from the enemy against them from the north, or east, or both. Furthermore it now appeared that if the enemy gained the high ground on Skeheenahaine Hill (north west of the ambush site) the volunteers would be unable to withdraw to the north west which was the obvious route open to them, as they were aware at this stage of enemy troops to the west, south, north east and east. Liam Deasy and those in Mick Crowley's section "C" had no idea of the strength of the forces attacking Tom Kellehers section "F".

Had the enemy been successful in over running that section and taking the high ground at the rear of the ambush column, then the losses incurred by the volunteers in fighting their way north could have been serious. This route had to be kept open.

Local knowledge was vital here. Liam ordered Spud Murphy, second in command of Crowley's section, to take the six most experienced men in the section to reinforce Kelleher's section. His instructions were to line the fence, where the enemy's thrust was the greatest, and to ensure that the younger men already there (and under fire for the first time) were standing at the fence and firing into the enemy.

Spud Murphy led this group, which included Eugene "Nudge" Callanan, Derry O'Callaghan (Newcestown) and Paddy O'Sullivan (Kilbrittain) to Kellehers aid. Spud had been wounded a week before in an attack on the police at Rosscarbery and had his right arm in a sling. He placed this section under the command of Tom Kelleher and they did much to stem the enemy's attempts to gain the high ground and surround the column. Had the attempt succeeded then the volunteers could well have been annihalated. Denis Lordan on his own initiative also dispatched two men - Captain Denis Mehigan (Bandon) and Captain Con Lehane (Timoleague) - to the aid of Tom Kelleher as his (Lordan's) section was not yet engaged with the enemy.

Tom Kelleher was captain of the local company and of course had expert knowledge of the area and the terrain around Crossbarry. His section was to guard the column's left flank and rear. He was in position (F1 on map) covering the Quarry road from Ballincollig. The British troops left the quarry road and advanced up O'Driscolls old road, to get behind the rear flank of the column. Now Kelleher was confronted by a vastly superior force approaching in extended order down O'Driscolls old road to O'Driscolls farmhouse. Some of the troops went around the back of the farmhouse and across a field towards Liam, and obviously making for the high ground on Skeheenahaine Hill. No one knew better than Kelleher, that if the British succeeded in gaining the hill that the only line of withdrawal open to the Column would be sealed off, and any attempts to fight their way through could only result in almost total annihilation of the Column. This enemy force had to be stopped at all cost.

Tom Kelleher realised at once that his small group (14 men) could not withstand a frontal attack from this superior force. He did not know that Deasy had dispatched reinforcements under "Spud" Murphy to help him. Thinking that he and his men were on their own to stop this enemy movement, Kelleher - the great tactician that he was, laid his own traps for the enemy. As can be seen on the accompanying map, across the stream to the left of Kellehers position were the ruins of Ballyhandle Castle in what is a large undulating field. He now dispatched two men, Dan Mehigan (Captain of the Bandon Company) and Con Lehane (Captain of the Timoleague Company) to the ruins with orders to hold their fire until the enemy, who were approaching the ruins from behind O'Driscolls farm, were well into the open field and then to shoot the officer leading the advance. While the advance guard of this detachment were moving towards the castle ruins, Kellehers section opened fire on the main body of troops who were advancing across the valley (from O'Driscolls old road) with the obvious intention of joining up again with the detachment who skirted behind the farmhouse.

Meanwhile Mehigan and Lehane in the castle ruins carried out Kelleher's orders to the letter, and allowed the advance group to come within twenty yards of their position and then opened fire. The enemy officer, a Captain Hotblack of Major Percival's infamous staff, was shot dead in front of the castle, and of the 30 N.C.O.'s and men in his platoon many were killed or wounded. The rest ran back to shelter in disarray. Kelleher's plan had worked brilliantly.

By this time "Spud" Murphy and his reinforcements had arrived to strengthen Kelleher's force and the enemy were stopped in their tracks. This was a decisive action in the battle. Had the troops left the old road sooner what would have happened?. In the course of the action Jim Crowley of Ballinadee was wounded by a dum-dum bullet above the knee and was invalided for life as a result. John O'Leary of Kilbrittain picked him up and carried him to safety.

7th Action

Having dispatched "Spud" Murphy and reinforcements to support Kelleher, the Brigade Adj. Liam Deasy, now left Crowley's Section "C" and proceeded to sections "A" & "B" where the fourth action had taken place and where now the men of these sections (on the orders of Tom Barry) were gathering up the arms and ammunition captured from those troops in the ambushed lorries . The ammunition was very welcome, as each volunteer had had only forty rounds each at the beginning of the action and much of this had been expended. Tom Barry ordered the bodies of the British troops, some dead in the lorries and on the road, some dead in the field south of the road, to be gathered together and placed away from the lorries, and then he ordered the lorries to be burned.

Liam Deasy told him of the new phase of the battle (the shooting at the rear) that he, Barry, could not have heard with the firing that had been going on around him, and of the steps he (Deasy) had taken to reinforce Kelleher's position.

After quick consultation, the Column commanders decision was that the Brigade Adj should take sections "A", "B", "C" and "G" at all speed to Skeheenahaine Hill, a quarter of a mile to the rear of these sections, and get control of the hill before the enemy could. Meanwhile, the Column commander would go first to the relief of Kelleher, and then bring Kearney's, Lordan's and Kelleher's sections ("D","E"and"F"), out to join them on Skeheenahaine hill. The agreed signal for withdrawal was to be two blasts of his whistle.

Liam Deasy and the main body saw the lorries on fire and, with the arms collected (one Lewis gun and ten pans of ammo, rifles and ammo) they retired at the double up Harold's old road across two fields under cover of fences and took up position at Skeheenahaine minutes after leaving the ambush positions. He now surveyed the situation from the high ground and had an excellent view of the south, east and north east. They waited for the arrival of Tom Barry and the sections "D", "E", and "F".

Now for the first time firing was heard coming from the direction of Crossbarry village almost three quarters of a mile away. It was obvious that a third force of enemy was now advancing from the south east and were engaged by Kearney and Lordan's sections ("D" & "E"). Seconds later a fourth force (under the command of Major A.E. Percival) of 30-40 troops at the double, were observed due east towards Killeens (Hartnetts) and were advancing extended over two - three fields in front of Hartnetts farm, with the intention of getting behind both Kearney's and Lordan's sections to surround them. Had they been able to cross the Crossbarry-Begley's Forge road 300-400 yards ahead of them, they would have succeeded and the result would have been fatal to the men of these two sections. To stop them was imperative.

Deasy ordered the 60 men now at Skeheenahaine to line the fence facing east and fire three rounds of independent fire at 1200 yards. Though the possibility of hitting any of the enemy was almost nil, they, the enemy, would know that they faced a strong force and they might be wary of continuing their action at their present speed. The effect was fantastic. Not alone did they stop in their tracks, they about-faced and raced for the protection of Hartnetts yard and the surrounding fences. They did not appear again during the time the volunteers held Skeheenahaine hill. Ten minutes later the Column commander arrived with Kellehers section and the wounded Jim Crowley.

8th Action
Denis Lordan's Section "E" was first attacked from the Crossbarry-Dunkeareen road immediately in front of his position, and then from Crossbarry bridge and from the Kileens area. These were the enemy forces from Cork and Kinsale respectively. His position was the most exposed of the ambush positions and his men were behind a very low fence with rising ground behind them, making any withdrawal extremely hazardous over open ground. Even to gain the comparative safety of Beasley's garden, and then the previously agreed withdrawal route up Harolds old road, they would have to cover almost three hundred yards along a very low ditch. The volley from Skeheenahaine

was clearly heard by the men in Section "E" and the enemy fire from the Kileens direction ceased immediately thus giving them some relief. Nevertheless, Lordan felt it would still be extremely tricky to withdraw from their position as they were still under fire from the Dunkeereen road and Crossbarry bridge, yet to remain in this position was even more risky as Lordan realised they would be cut off by the enemy troops. He made the decision to withdraw. Two of his men, Jerh. O'Leary and Con Daly had been killed, Dan Corcoran was wounded and Peter "Scottie" Monahan, fatally wounded, had died next to Lordan.

Peter "Scottie" Monahan, a Scotsman of Irish parentage (his mother was from Mallow) was a deserter from the Cameron Highlanders stationed at Cobh in East Cork. He was a Sergeant in the Royal Engineers attached to the Camerons.

The mine at "E" section failed to detonate and while checking it out he was shot and wounded. He became entangled in the wires from the plunger to the mine in endeavouring to detonate it. He was again shot in the lower abdomen and while writhing in agony on the ground he became totally entangled in the wires. Peter "Scottie" Monahan is buried in the Republican Plot in St. Patricks cemetary in Bandon. My father was visited by his relatives in the 1960s.

The decision to withdraw having been made there was no time to lose, Lordan ordered Mick Kearney to look after the badly wounded Dan Corcoran when he gave the signal to break out of their position, and while still engaging the enemy he went to move Peter Monahan's body so that he could detach and retrieve the plunger from the wires around the body. Just then he saw Pete Kearney standing on the fence of Beasley's garden waving at him to withdraw. Kearney had heard the pre-arranged signal for withdrawal (namely two blasts on the Column Commanders whistle) which Lordan had not heard due to his own and the enemy fire. Now luck favoured the volunteers once more in the fight because Lordan, in the act of moving Monahans body, slipped and accidentally touched the plunger with his arm and detonated the mine on the road.

The explosion took the enemy by surprise and sent a huge cloud of dust and earth into the air. Under cover of this accidental good fortune, Lordan and his men made a run for the safety of Beasley's garden and he led them, with Dan Corcoran (and the plunger), up Harolds old road and up to Skeheenahaine by the route taken by the main body of Volunteers and joined them about twenty five minutes after they had arrived there.

Dan Corcoran was attended to by Dr. Con Lucey (the Brigade medical officer), assisted by Eugene "Nudge" Callanan, as had been Jimmy Crowley earlier.

9th Action

Now the full Column (minus the three dead, Peter Monahan, Jerh. O'Leary and Con Daly) was assembled at Skeheenahaine Hill, but they were far from safe yet. They had been attacked from three sides . Only from the north west were they so far free from attack, but it was a certainty by now that they were in a position surrounded on all sides. It was essential that they gain the safety of the higher ground of Raheen Hill about two miles north, the highest ground in the area.

There were quick consultations between Deasy, Barry and Kelleher (local Column Captain) whose knowledge of the terrain proved of paramount importance. It was decided that Deasy, would take the main body of men directly, by the shortest route, to Raheen Hill and to hold it if attacked by the force from the north that had not yet been encountered but whom all felt to be out there somewhere. Tom Barry, with Captain Tom Kelleher would bring the rearguard of twenty five men and four wounded, two of them seriously, by a circuituous route to Raheen Hill. The Battle of Crossbarry was over.

One hundred and four Volunteers, young men who had left their families and homes behind them to ensure that you reader, and I, our generations and generations to follow, would not have to live beneath the yoke of British creulty and oppression as had our people for the previous seven hundred years. Farmer's sons, farm workers, shop assistants, clerical workers, medical students, stood shoulder to shoulder against the greatest British force ever put in the field against the I.R.A. during the War of Independence. Some of these Volunteers were under fire for the first time but they and every other man in the Column displayed gallantry and courage for which in any army in the world they would have been honoured and decorated.

Three brave Volunteers had given their lives for Ireland at Crossbarry that day: Con Daly of Ballinascarthy, Jeremiah O'Leary of Leap and Peter "Scottie" Monahan (which was not his real name). All three were interred in the Republican Plot in St. Patrick's Cemetery in Bandon.

The Withdrawal

The Column withdrawal from Crossbarry began. The following is the account of that withdrawal by the man (Batt Foley), who guided the Column to it's destination at Gurranereagh.

On the evenning of Crossbarry Ambush the Column retreated through Rearour, Curragh, Upper Scart to Knockawaddra where they rested for a few hours in the local houses, making Headquarters at Lawrence O'Leary's Kilbonane. All the men had a meal of some kind before starting out at nightfall for Gurranereagh where they were to be billeted for the night (the men had not eaten since the previous evening). The shortest possible route was twenty miles via by-roads.

After leaving Kilbonane the Column proceeded through Rathcullen via Parkmore Cross on to Rathfilane. When they reached Rathfilane scouts reported that the Military / Auxiliaries from Macroom were at Foley's Cross, Carrigeen (on the main Macroom - Bandon road) a mile further West on the road the Column was to travel. The Column then left the direct route and turned left to Rathfilane Lane in which it took up positions for a short time until the all clear was given. The Column then proceeded through Ballinguila, Kilbrennan, turning right at Strawhall Cross and keeping the old road to Crookstown for approximately 100 yards, they turned left at Halloran's boreen Carrigeen, to the main Bandon - Macroom road (where the enemy had been earlier that night) and travelled for half a mile before turning over Hickey's Bridge to proceed along a by-road West. This road was about half a mile south of Crookstown Village on the main Crookstown / Quarries Cross road at Belmont.

At this stage the Column turned left and proceeded for about quarter of a mile in a southerly direction towards Quarries Cross. The next turn was to the right through the Commons mountain via Ardra and out on the main Bealnablath / Mossgrove road on top of Murray's Hill (this was a cart passage in the furze) then right (down from) Murray's Hill and out at Bealnablath on the Cork - Bantry road. It turned West for Poularick, on to Horn Hill and direct to Bengour to the right of Gurranereagh where the men were billeted.

In his account Batty mentions that Lawrence O'Leary's was the Headquarters while the Column rested and were fed and, while this was so, it is obvious that no one family could have sufficient supplies on hand to feed nearly one hundred men who suddenly appeared at their door.

This is where Tadg O'Sullivan, the Column Quartermaster took over. He went to a number of houses in the area and asked the housewife in each to put her largest pot on the fire and to boil as much home-cured bacon as it would hold. He dispatched other men to collect bread, butter and eggs and when all was gathered from the ever-generous people, the Volunteers banished the hunger of their long fast (it was now 3.30 p.m. and, although they had not eaten since the previous evening, they had fought and won, a murderous battle for their very survival against a vastly superior enemy). The Column then continued to Gurranereagh as Batty described above.

Batty Foley

On reaching their goal, headquarters was set up in Joe O'Sullivan's and the men of the West Cork Flying Column, weary but proud, were directed to their billets.Throughout the entire march from Raheen to Gurranereagh the Column was in danger of ambush. The need to maintain flanking sections, a vanguard and a rearguard was essential.

It was on the following day that they got confirmation of the death of their Brigade Commanding Officer Charlie Hurley, and heard of his gallant fight and death, at Denny Forde's on the morning of Crossbarry. On the following day, Monday, the extra men who had joined the Column for the ambush at Shippool were stood down and returned to their own Companies. That night the Column now at it's normal strenght of forty men, marched to Ahiohill and on the Tuesday night on to Clogagh for the funeral of Charlie Hurley.

Liam Deasy describes the sad occassion in his book (Towards Ireland Free):

> *The funeral procession left Clogagh church in the early hours (2 a.m.) of Wednesday morning, 23rd March, and was led by the local curate to the family burial place. The Column acted as guard of honour and Flor Begley who had played warlike tunes at Crossbarry a few days previously, now played the Dead March.*

> *It was a scene never to be forgotten by those present — the flickering lights of the swaying lanterns, the slow tramp of the Column, the sobbing*

of bereaved relatives, and the sad notes of the warpipes — all in the dark chilly hours before the dawn of a morning in March. When the lonely graveyard was reached, the last prayers were recited and the soldiers' last honours were paid to one of Ireland's most faithful and bravest sons.

Shortly after the withdrawal had started Liam Deasy drew the attention of Flor Begley to smoke rising from the direction of Forde's farm (where the Brigade O.C. Charlie Hurley, had been kiled) with the comment "they have started reprisals Flor, they have set fire to Forde's house". Begley (who had been staying at Fordes with Charlie for the previous few months, it being Brigade Headquarters at that time) looked back and said "no Liam, it is not the house it is a feore of oats that they have set fire to and there are Mills bombs hidden in it". This indeed was the case but, under the very noses of the soldiers Mary Forde removed them from there and hid them a well. That fire was only the beginning of the British reprisals for their defeat at Crossbarry. Over the next days they burned farmhouses in the area and damaged a great amount of other property.

Among the houses burned were:
O'Mahony's of Belrose; Hartnett's of Killeens; O'Leary's of Ballyhandle; and Kelleher's of Crow Hill.

Military experts might argue against the advisability of operating a column of over a hundred lightly armed men (such as the West Cork Flying Column), without reinforcements against vastly superior forces. There were two reasons why this had to be.
1. The Brigade had no more arms. If it had there would have been many more columns of equal strength formed.
2. To divide the Brigade Flying Column into smaller columns would have seriously reduced its effectiveness. Since the previous Autumn, because the enemy now only moved out of their barracks in large numbers, a smaller unit of the I.R.A would have been useless against such numbers. Nor, as Crossbarry exemplified, could they have defended themselves successfully if surprised in any of the large scale round-ups which were carried out since the beginning of the year.

You may wonder how it happened that the Column of one hundred and four men, outnumbered almost ten to one by a vastly superior force and almost completely surrounded, could achieve such a victory. There are a number of reasons why the British suffered their greatest defeat in Ireland during the War of Independence at Crossbarry on that crisp March day.

The fourth most important reason was the failure of the British to surround the Column completely. This was because the one hundred and twenty Auxiliaries who set out from Macroom to participate in the roundup went to Kilbarry instead of to Crossbarry. This left the North - North West segment of the encirclement uncompleted and this was the route by which the Column were able to break out. Had the Auxiliaries arrived to close that gap the likelihood is that the Column would have been annihilated.

The third reason was that the while the British were not aware that the Column was at Crossbarry the Column were made aware of the British presence in the area at 2.30 a.m. by the lights and noise of their lorries coming from the direction of Bandon. This gave the Column the advantage of surprise over their enemies. This had a telling effect on the battle that followed.

The second reason can be summed up in one word, morale. Here was a fighting unit with a strong belief in their cause, acutely aware of their own capabilities and with calm confidence in their leaders and in each other. Napolean said "in war it is not men who count, it is the man". He was referring to leaders but, at Crossbarry his observation could be applied to every single man of the Column.

But the first reason was leadership.

On that great day when the first crack in the mighty British Empire was caused, Liam Deasy, Tom Barry and Section Commanders Sean Hales, John Lordan, Mick Crowley, Pete Kearney, Denis Lordan, Tom Kelleher and Christy O'Connell provided the leadership which was so necessary for that momentous victory.

The official account of British casulties was thirty nine soldiers killed, including five officers, and forty seven wounded. It is reliably estimated that the British losses were far greater.

It is interesting to note that three of the British troops at Crossbarry were awarded medals for bravery shown on that day, they were:

Acting Sergeant B. Loftus, 1155 (MT) Coy., R.A.S.C. His citation reads, "This N.C.O. shewed great gallantry and initiative in leading men during an ambush on March 19th, 1921. He also made repeated attempts, under heavy fire to rescue a wounded officer lying in an exposed position."

Acting Sergeant A. Mepham, 1155 (MT) Coy., R.A.S.C. His citation reads, "During an ambush on a convoy of several lorries, the Crown Forces sustained heavy casulties and were forced to leave their lorries and retire on a small farm. Sergeant Mepham seeing the officer in charge of the convoy and several others lying wounded in exposed positions, made his way back to the lorries and drove off one in which he took all the wounded to a place of safety".

Sergeant   M.M. Poole, 1st Essex Regiment, His citation reads, "Sergeant Poole displayed gallantry in leading a party of young soldiers in action on 19th March, 1921. He also made repeated attempts to bring in a wounded officer lying in an exposed position, under heavy fire".

After the Battle of Crossbarry, according to Lord Birkenhead (Lord Chancellor) it was beginning to dawn on Lloyd George that the Irish Resistance was a very real force which had to be met by methods other than by force.

The Battle of Crossbarry had broken the resolve of the British Government and they now sued for peace. On July 11th 1921 a truce was declared.

The War of Independence was at an end.

BIOGRAPHICAL NOTES

Charlie Hurley

Charlie Hurley was born on the 19th March 1894 and was shot dead by British forces on the 19th March 1921. A native of Baurleigh, Kilbrittain, he joined the Volunteers in 1915 while employed at Haulbowline Dockyard. He took up employment in Castletownbere in 1917 and was very active in the Volunteer Movement in that area. In 1918 he was arrested and was charged with having plans for the defence of the Beara Peninsula in his posession. He was convicted and sentenced to five years penal servitude. When released on ticket-of leave in October 1919 he joined the Kilbrittain Company of the Volunteers. In january 1920 he was appointed Vice-Commandant of the Bandon Battalion and became Commanding Officer of the Brigade in July following the arrest of Tom Hales.

His first decision as Brigade O.C. was to form a Brigade Column which, under the leadership of Tom Barry became the renowned West Cork Flying Column. This decision of Charlie Hurley changed the the whole manner in which the struggle for independence was fought and was to prove decisive to the outcome of that struggle. As Brigade Commandant he was in charge of the following engagements:

- Ahawadda (Timoleague) Ambush.
- Inishannon Bridge Ambush.
- Kilbrittain Barracks Attack.
- Raid on British Naval Stores in Castletownbere.
- Raid on British Patrol Boat in Castletownbere.
- Second Attack on Howes Strand Coastguard Station.
- Upton Train Ambush.
- Leap Ambush.

He was also in command at the attempted ambushes at: Fanlobbus (Dunmanway), Carrigmore (Enniskeane), Palace Anne (Enniskeane),

Kilbrittain, Farnahoe, Ballinadee, and in the Bandon area, at Tinker's Cross, Laragh, Kilpatrick, Newcestown, Mawbeg and Mallowgaton.

At Upton Train Ambush (February 1921), he was wounded when a bullet entered behind his right ear and came out at the left side of his nose. He also sprained his ankle very badly when jumping from the bridge at that ambush. On the morning of March 19th 1921, while convalescing at Humphrey Forde's in Ballymurphy (near Crossbarry), the house was surrouded by the british and in trying to escape, this gallant leader was killed. He was buried in Clogagh Cemetary in the dead of night with full military honours.

Liam Deasy, Brigade Adjutant

Liam Deasy was born in 1896 at Kilmacsimon Quay, Co. Cork, just a few miles from where the Battle of Kinsale was fought in 1601. His parents, both of whom came from nationalist backgrounds, instilled a love of country and of Irish culture in Liam and his five brothers. In those days prior to the advent of radio, the evenings in most houses were spent seated around the fire listening to the tales of heroism of previous generations. It was no wonder then that Liam should have absorbed a strong feeling of pride in his counry's heritage.

At the age of thirteen years he came to Bandon to find employment and here he joined the Gaelic Athletic Association (G.A.A.), and later the Gaelic League (for the revival and preservation of the Irish language as it was not allowed to be taught in the schools then). His activities in the G.A.A. occupied a huge amount of his time. He founded and played with the Valley Rovers Hurling and Football Club at Innishannon, a village four miles to the east of Bandon.

In 1918 Liam Deasy formed a Volunteer Company in Innishannon and was selected as its first Captain and because of his organisational and adminstrative abilities his rise through the ranks of the Volunteers was very rapid. By August 1919 he was Brigade Adjutant and under his guidance the Brigade became a model of military effiency and acheivement. After the death of his comrade and Commanding Officer Charlie Hurley, he was appointed Brigade Commandant.

In the Civil War which followed our victory over our British oppressors Liam took the side of the Volunteers against the Treaty.

In later years he founded the Dunloe Men's Clothing Co. in Cork City and was joined in that company by some of his former comrades . During the Emergency declared in this country at the outbreak of World War 2 (1939--1945), Liam with many of his former comrades including Tom Crofts, Mossie Donegan and Florrie O'Donoghue enlisted as privates in the regular army. Once again his adminstrative prowess came to the fore by January 1941 he was Command Staff Officer, Southern Command and from October 1942 he was Staff Officer, Office of Director L.D.F. (Local Defence Force, the precurser of the F.C.A.). In the words of Major General Costello (General commanding the 1st Division) "Liam Deasy would have been said to have been from the beginning the organiser of the L.D.F. in Munster and this was infinitely better organised and prepared for war than the L.D.F. elsewhere. He was outstandingly gifted as an organiser, had immense prestige and was an outstanding judge of men."

Liam Deasy died in 1974.

Tom Barry, Column Commandant

Here was a man who was a legend in his own time. The son of an R.I.C. man, Tom Barry was born in Killorglin, Co. Kerry on 1st July 1897. His father left the R.I.C. in 1901 and after a number of years in business in Rosscarbery, Co. Cork the family moved. to Convent Hill in Bandon.

In June 1915, at almost 18 years of age, Tom Barry joined the British Army and was posted to Mesopotamia, there to fight against the German-Turk alliance. He rose to the rank of Bombardier. Demobilised in 1919, he returned to Bandon where he joined the British Legion. In 1920, Tom and a friend were beaten up by British military and the following morning the hot headed Tom approached the I.R.A. to offer his services in the fight for freedom. His offer was treated with great suspicion for over six weeks. Having been interviewed twice by Brigade Officers he was finally accepted and appointed training officer to the Brigade.

Tom Barry was a leader of men, all of whom would have followed him to hell and back which is more than the soldiers of General Macready would do for him. When Tom was appointed Training Officer of the Third Cork Brigade the War of Independence in Ireland took a new direction. It is true that he was short tempered, uncompromising and ruthless but he was above all a leader and the men of the Flying Column responded to his leadership. The successes of the Flying Column under Tom Barry's leadership are well documented in Liam Deasy's "Towareds Ireland Free" and Barry's own book "Guerilla Days in Ireland". In the Civil War he took the side of the Republicans.

Tom Barry died in 1980.

Sean Hales, Commander Section 'A'

Sean Hales was born in 1881 at Knocknacurra, near Bandon and was the son of Robert Hales, The Lough, Clohane and Margaret Fitzgerald of Gortnacrusha. Robert was a Fenian and Margaret was from a very nationalist background as well so it is no wonder that Sean, his four brothers and four sisters were all active in the War of Independence. He was a big man standing over six feet tall and built accordingly. As well as his brothers, of whom Bob was an international runner, Sean was also a fine athlete excelling at weight throwing. He played hurling and football with the Valley Rovers Club in Innishannon.

He joined the Volunteers in 1914 as a member of the Ballinadee Company and was very active throughout the entire period 1915 to1921. He escaped capture by the R.I.C. in dramatic fashion in May 1918 as recorded in Liam Deasy's book "Towards Ireland Free" and was "on the run" from that time to the end of hostilities on July 1921. He participated in the attack on Timoleague Barracks, the engagements at Brinny and Newcestown, in the abduction of Lord Bandon and of course, he was a Section-Commander at the Battle of Crossbarry.

In the Civil War Sean took the Pro-Treaty side. He was shot in Dublin in 1922.

John Lordan, Commander Section 'B'

John Lordan was born on the Lordan family farm at Coolanagh, Newcestown in 1881. He was the eldest of a family of six children. He had one brother and four sisters. His father and his uncle were both "on the run". British Forces surrounded their home in the hope of arresting them and on discovering that they were not there they ransacked the house and then burned it down. John was arrested in 1919 and with his comrade Charlie, Hurley was jailed in Wormwood Scrubs Prison in London. On his release he was again active with the Volunteers and at the ambush at Kilmichael in November 1920 he was wounded. At the Battle of Crossbarry John was a Section-Commander in charge of Section 'B' and this Section was the first to engage the enemy on that fateful day.

John took the Anti-Treaty side in the Civil War. during which he was captured and spent some time in Cork Gaol. After the end of hostilities he returned home to Coolanagh and in 1926 and married Sissy Canty. They had three children, a boy and two girls. John was a Fianna Fail member of Cork County Council. Tragically in 1930, he died of a burst appendix and left a grieving wife and three young children.

Mick Crowley, Commander Section 'C'

Mick Crowley was born on the outskirts of Kilbrittain village in Co. Cork. He had three brothers and two sisters all of whom were involved in the War of Independence. Because of their known nationalistic ideals the family suffered more than most at the hands of the British forces. While they lived just outside the village, their mother owned another business in the village next door to the R.I.C. Barracks. As a result of the family's activities in the Volunteer movement their home was burned to the ground by the military. Their shop however, was not burned down as the military feared that the fire might spread to the R.I.C. Barracks next door, but it was demolished stone by stone. Men from the village and the surrounding area were forced at gunpoint to level the building.

Mick's brother Patrick was killed by British forces at Maryboro on February 4th 1921.

Mick emigrated to America after the War of Independence and there he qualified as an engineer. He later returned to Ireland and worked as an engineer with Sligo Co. Council until his death.

Peter Kearney, Commander Section 'D'

Peter Kearney was born in Lettergorman, Dunmanway, Co. Cork on June 17th 1899 and he died in Dublin on November 14th 1968. He joined the Volunteer Company in University College Cork in 1918 when he commenced his studies in Medicine. In February of 1921 he transferred from the College I.R.A. Company to the West Cork Flying Column and took part in the attacks on Bandon, Innishannon, Skibbereen and Drimoleague. At Crossbarry he was a Section-Commander and his gallantry and his leadership inspired the men in his section.

Another side of Pete Kearney often referred to by his comrades in arms was his ability to cheer them up on the long route marches or in uncomfortable billets with his repertoire of marching songs and ballads which he sang in his own inimitable style.

In 1924 he went to America and worked in the Insurance industry in New York. While there he met his future wife Peg, who grew up North of Dunmanway, less than ten miles from his home in Lettergorman. He always wanted to return to Ireland, and came back in 1933 to Dublin. He married Peg in 1934 and they had two sons, both of whom are engineers. Pete joined the South of Ireland Asphalt Company on his arrival in Ireland and was in charge of their Asphalt Department from that time until his death in 1968. He was widely known and respected throughout the Irish construction industry.

Being based in Dublin he was very helpful in securing pensions and other help for many of those affected by the War of Independence. In the

1950's and 60's he was very active in bringing together both sides of the Civil War and organised an Annual Retreat in Milltown for veterans to help this process of reconcilation. He was also a member of the original committee for the restoration of Kilmainham Jail and was active in other commemoration projects.

Outside of work he enjoyed a game of golf despite a stiff knee esulting from his activities in 1921 and he attended all the major matches in Croke Park. He loved a sing song and his rendering of "Lament of an Irish Maiden" (Carrigdhoun) and other Irish songs were the high point of many an evening. Although he lived in Dublin he looked forward each year to his holidays in West Cork

Denis Lordan, Commander Section 'E'

Denis Lordan was the only child of Daniel and Hanna (nee O'Neill) Lordan. He was born in May 1898 in Maryboro, Timoleague. His parents (farmers) both died before he was six years old. The young Denis went to live with an aunt in Kinsale and during the school holidays would return to Ardacrow, Kilbrittain to his uncle and cousins.

In 1912 a Sluagh of Fianna Eireann was formed in Kinsale and he was one of the six members. This branch of Fianna Eireann lasted but a year and in1914, when the Volunteers started in Kinsale, Denis joined the movement. It was with dificulty he was accepted as he was only just sixteen years of age.

In 1915 he went to live with his uncle in Ardacrow and joined the the newly formed Kilbrittain Volunteer Company. In 1916 this Company got stronger with the help of the Ballinadee Company and denis became dedicated to the cause of freedom. He did stalwart work for the Kilbrittain Company, the Brigade and laterly for the Flying Column. At Crossbarry he was Section-Commander of the eastern end of the ambush position (Section "E"), an exposed and dangerous position from which withdrawal was very difficult.

In 1923 he went to the Argentine where he worked for nine years and became fluent in Spanish. He loved the Irish language and was an avid G.A.A. supporter although he never excelled on the field. He returned to

Ireland in 1932 and joined his old comrade Liam Deasy at the Dunloe Men's Clothing Company (later known as Ideal Weatherproof) in Cork. He remained with that Company until he retired in 1968.

During the Emergency 1939 - 45, he rose to the rank of Captain in the Army. In 1935 he married Christina O'Regan and they had two children, a boy and a girl. He was associated with the group who founded Garryvoe Summer Irish College (the foreruner of Scoil-na-nOg Glanmire), and was a member of Cork Chamber of Commerce, The Spanish Circle and Kinsale golf Club. Denis Lordan died in 1978.

Tom Kelleher, Commander Section 'F'

Born into a family with a strong Republican tradition at Crowhill, Upton, in September 1895, Tom Kelleher was one of ten children. His father John Kelleher, a native of Killmichael, was a renowned athlete. His mother Mary McCarthy, of Innishannon, was related to William Philip Allin one of the famed Manchester Martyrs.

Tom attended school in Knockavilla where he was also influenced by the nationalistic outlook of his teacher Tim O'Connor. It was not surprising then that when Bob Walsh the local Organiser of the Volunteers, asked him if he would be interested in joining young Tom gave a positive response and was enlisted in the Crosspound Company. Much of his time up to 1920 was devoted to drilling and training in the use of arms. In October of that year he was one of a number of Volunteers under the command of Seán Hales who engaged the British at Newcestown. This was to be the first of many confrontations that Tom Kelleher had with the British forces of occupation.

The next major engagement, the Upton Train Ambush (February 1921) was to be one that stamped Tom as a man of undoubted courage, ability and leadership qualities, exemplified by his rescue of the injured Charlie Hurley Brigade O.C., whom he carried on his back to safety under heavy gunfire. The following month he was a Section Commander at the Battle of Crossbarry. The part played in that decisive battle by Tom Kelleher's Section proved crucial to the outcome the complete rout of British forces who outnumbered the 104 Volunteers by almost ten to one. He took part in a number of other engagements up to the Truce (July 1921) notably, the attack on Rosscarbery R.I.C. Barracks. During the Truce he took over Kinsale Barracks from the infamous Major Percival. He fought on the Republican side during the Civil War.

In July 1937 he married Sile Crowley, Belrose, Upton, a member of another staunch Repulican family. There were four children of this union. In 1952 the Kelleher family sold their home at Crowhill and moved to Passage West. On retiring from farming in 1972 Tom and Sile went to live in the Cork City surburb of Ballintemple.

A devoted family man, a good conversationalist and storyteller, a wielder of the caman in his youth with Valley Rovers, an accomplished step dancer, Tom Kelleher enjoyed life to the full. He loved to meet old comrades and friends and enjoyed making new ones. He was a committed Republican throughout his life and up to the time of his death in 1985 he longed to see a united Ireland.

Christy O'Connell, Commander Section 'G'

Born in Eyeries, on the Beara Penninsula, on September 3rd 1896, Christy O'Connell was one of eight children. His parents were nationalistic in outlook and like so many other families, suffered because of this. They lived over their business in Eyeries but when their house was commandeered by the British their business was severely damaged.

Christy joined the Volunteers at an early age and he led the very first attack on an R.I.C. Barracks in the 3rd Cork Brigade area when, on St. Patrick's Day 1918, he and a party of Volunteers from Eyeries, attacked and captured the local barracks. Later that year he was involved in the attack on the R.I.C. Barracks in Allihies. He was very active in his area and indeed in adjoining Company areas. He was also in the attack on Ballycrovane Coastguard Station and at the Battle of Crossbarry he was a Section Commander.

He took the anti-Treaty side in the Civil War and when it was ended he emigrated to America like so many of his comrades. There he worked for the Bell Telephone Company until the Wall Street stock market crash in 1929. He returned to Ireland in1937 where he married Nora O'Neill, also from Eyeries. There they ran the local Post Office and reared their family in the peace for which he had so gallantly fought.

Christy O'Connell retired in the late 1960's and he died in 1978.

Eugene Callanan, Assistant Brigade M.O.
Eugene Callanan was born on the 14th Nov. '98. His father Eugen was Secretary to Cork Co. Council and the family had a long assocation in local Government. They lived on Magazine Road in the Lough Parish. As a medical student in U.C.C. in the 1920's Eugene joined the College Company of the I.R.A. In December 1920 himself and his close friend Peter Kearney left their studies to join the Brigade Flying Column. He figured prominently in the Crossbarry Ambush and many other engagements. He was appointed a member of the Brigade Officer staff and was assistant Brigade Medical Officer to  Con Lucey. Having resumed his Medical Studies after the National struggle he played Inter Varsity hurling and football winning three Fitzgibbon and Sigerson Cup medals. After graduation he played with Collegians, Cork and Munster winning a hurling Railway Cup medal 1926 and Munster Senior Football medal in 1928.

Even though Gaelic Games were his first love he was a keen golfer, angler and general all round sportsman. He captained Bandon Golf Club in 1947, served as president in '53, '69 and '76 and was made an honourary life member. He was also interested in greyhound racing. He bred many a good dog and had a nomination for the Irish Cup at Clounanna.

His professional career commitment was in the Public Service where for over half a century he served as Dispensary Doctor, first at Innishannon and then Bandon. Neither time nor distance mattered in the service of the community.

His renowned wit, cheery manner, good humour and hearty laugh coupled with a fine singing voice enlivened many a gathering and endeared him to all who knew him.

Flor Begley, "The Piper of Crossbarry"

Born in 1898 at Castle Road, Bandon. Co Cork. Flor Begley was one of seven children, two girls and five boys. He received his education at Mr. Murphy's National School after which he went to work in the Bandon Hosiery Company. He joined the Gaelic League in 1914 and in 1915 he joined the Volunteer unit in Bandon. This unit was connected to the Ballinadee Company as there was not a Volunteer Company in Bandon at that time. In early 1916 Flor and Pat Dwyer went to Headquarters to register the Bandon unit as a Volunteer Company. One of his brothers died when quite young but his other three brothers all played an active part in the War of Independence.

He was arrested in 1916 and was taken to Richmond Barracks in Dublin with many other Volunteers. When some of these pointed out (against Flor's wishes) that he was not yet 18 years old he was released. His companions were interned. In 1917 he formed the Volunteer Pipe Band (which later became the Third Cork Brigade Band). He collected money from far and wide to pay for the band instruments. By 1919 he was Acting Brigade Adjutant and on New Year's Day 1920 was arrested once again. This time he was incarcerated in Wormwood Scrubs Prison in London where he and the other Volunteers there, went on hunger-strike. When they were transferred to hospitals under guard they made their escape and made their way back to Ireland. In December 1920 his brother was killed by the Crown Forces.

On February 15th 1921 at Upton Station Flor had a very narrow escape from death and was again in the thick of things at the Battle of Crossbarry five weeks later where he marched up and down playing martial airs on his warpipes as the bullets flew past. It is for this that he will always be remembered as the "Piper of Crossbarry". He took the anti-Treaty side in the Civil War and like all others who did so, he suffered for it.

In 1923 he went into partnership with his friend Sean Buckley in Sean's newsagency business in Bandon. In 1924 he bought Sean's share of that business and today 75 years later, the business is being carried on by his son Diarmuid and his wife Elsie. In 1931 he married Anita Deasy from Ballineen and they had five children, four girls and a boy. Flor took an active part in the political life of the country through the Fianna Fail Cumann in Bandon and was again active for his country during the Emergency Years 1939-1945. Having lead the Volunteer Pipe Band at Feiseanna all over West Cork since its formation in 1917 he and his two fellow trustees handed over the band's instruments, on loan, to the newly formed Bandon F.C.A. Pipe Band in 1940, to be returned if that band was ever disbanbed. He was very involved in the G.A.A. and was one of the Trustees of the Charlie Hurley G.A.A. Stadium until his death.

Flor Begley died in 1979.

Third Cork Brigade Pipe Band, formed by Flor Begley in 1917.

THE BOYS OF KILMICHAEL

Whilst we honour in song and in story
The names of Pearse and Mc Bride
Whose names are illumined in glory
With martyrs who long since have died.

Chorus:
Forget not the Boys of Kilmichael
Those brave lads so gallant and true
Who fought ëneath the green flag of Erin
And conquered the Red, White and Blue.

On the 28th day of November,
The Tans left the town of Macroom,
They were armed in two Crossley tenders
Which led them into their doom;
They were on the road to Kilmichael
And never expected a stop,
There they met the Boys of the Column
Who made a clean sweep of them all.

Chorus;

The sun in the west it was sinking'
'Twas the eve of a cold Winter's day,
The Tans we were wearily waiting
Sailed into the spot where we lay;
And over the hills went the echo,
The sound of the rifle and gun,
And the flames from their lorries gave tidings
That the Boys from the Column had won.

Chorus;

The lorries were ours before twilight,
And high over Dunmanway town
Our banners in triumph were waving
To show that the Tans had gone down;
We gathered our rifles and bayonets,
And soon left the glen so obscure,
And never drew rein 'til we halted
At the far-away camp at Granure.

Chorus:
Forget not the Boys of Kilmichael
Those brave lads so gallant and true
Who fought ëneath the green flag of Erin
And conquered the Red, White and Blue.

A commemoration in the 1930s at the site of the Kilmichael ambush.

111

UPTON AMBUSH

Many homes are filled with sorrow and with sadness,
Many hearts are filled with anguish and with pain,
For old Ireland now she hangs her head in mourning,
For the men who fell at Upton for Sinn Fein.

Chorus:
Let the moon shine tonight along the valley,
Where those men who fought for freedom now are laid,
May they rest in peace those men who died for Ireland,
And who fell at Upton ambush for Sinn Fein.
Some were thinking of their mothers, wives and sweethearts,
More were thinking of their dear old Irish homes,
Do they think of how they drilled along the valley,
Or when they marched out from Cork City to their doom.

Chorus:

The morning cry rang out, "Fix Bayonets, "
And the gallant lads they fixed them for the fray,
Gallantly they fought and died for Ireland,
Around the lonely woods at Upton far away.

Chorus:

Volunteer Pipe Band at Clogagh Cemetery for the
second anniversary of the death of Charlie Hurley.

THE MEN WHO FOUGHT AT CROSSBARRY

Staff Officers;
Liam Deasy, Brigade Adjutant.
Tom Barry, Column Commandant.
Flor Begley, Asst. Brigade Adjutant.
Dr. Con Lucey, Brigade Medical Officer.
Eugene Callanan, Asst. Brigade Medical Officer.
Tadg O'Sullivan, Column Quartermaster.
Mick Crowley, Brigade Engineer (Section Commander).

First Battalion;

Ballinadee Company
Sean Hales, Knocknacurra (Section Commander).
William Hales, Knocknacurra.
Bob Hales, Knocknacurra.
Con O'Donoghue, Rathtrout.
Jack O'Donoghue, Rathtrout.
Denny O'Donoghue, Rathtrout.
Matt Healy, Rathtrout.
Jim Crowley, Kilanetig (wounded).
Tim Crowley, Horsehill.
Jack Corkery, Cloghane.

Kilbrittain Company;
John O'Leary, Howes Strand.
Denis Lordan, Maryboro (Secion Commander).
Peter Monahan, Bandon (killed).
Jack Roche, Kilbrittain.
Denny O'Brien, Clonbouig.
Paddy O'Sullivan, Glanduff.

Timoleague Company
Con Lehane, Timoleague.
John O'Driscoll, Timoleague.
Dan Minihane, Timoleague.
Con Murphy, Carhue.
Jim Hodnett, Carhue.
Mick Deasy.
Tim Keohane.

Barryroe Company
Bill Mc Carthy.
Dan Holland.
Michael Coleman.
Denis O'Sullivan.
Con Callanan.
Denis O'Brien, Butlerstown.

Clogagh Company
Paddy Dempsey.
Mick O'Donovan.
Dan O'Donovan, Burran South.
Dan O'Donovan, Clogagh.
Con Daly, Ballinascarthy (killed).

Bandon Company
Denis Mehigan, Dangan.
Mick Kearney, Bandon.
Bill Buckley, Bandon.
Con Mc Carthy, Bandon.

Mount Pleasant / Farnivane Company
Frank Hurley, Laragh, Bandon.
Con O'Brien, Laragh, Bandon.
Jeremiah O'Brien, Tullyglass.

Newcestown Company
John Lordan, Coolinagh (Section Commander).
Jim Lordan, Coolinagh.
Bill Desmond.
Dan Canty, Farnalough.
Stephen Staunton.
Jeremiah Desmond.
Denis O'Callaghan, Lauravoulta.
John O'Callaghan, Lauravoulta.
Denny O'Brien, Tullyglass.
Dan Corcoran, Bengour (wounded).

Kilpatrick Company
Jim Doyle, Kilmore.
Jer Doyle, Kilmore.
John crowley.

Crosspound Company
Tom Kelleher, Crow Hill, Upton (Section Commander).

Second Battalion;

Clonakilty Company
Jim "Spud" Murphy, Clonakilty (Section Commander)
Dan Nugent, Clonakilty.
Jack Barry, Clonakilty.

Ardfield Company
Con O'Leary, Brownstown, Ardfield.
Dan O'Sullivan Cahir.

Kilkernmore Company
Eugene Mc Sweeney, Castlefreke.
Jack Mc Sweeney, Castlefreke.

Third Battalion;

Aultagh Company
John O'Donovan, Aultagh.

Clubhouse Company
Peter Kearney, Lettergorm (Section Commander).
Patsy O'Connell, Edencurra, Dunmanway.
Pat O'Donovan Nedinagh.

Behagh Company
Mick Hurley, Gortnamuckly, Dunmanway.

Knockbue Company
Denis O'Leary, Drimoleague.

Fourth Battalion;

Corran Company
Jeremiah O'Leary, Corran, Leap (killed).

Drinagh Company
Jack Dempsey, Dromindy.

Bredagh Company
Tim J. McCarthy, Lissane, Drimoleague.

Baltimore Company
Sean O'Neill, Baltimore.

Fifth Battalion;

Coomhola Company
Michael O'Driscoll, Snave, Bantry.
Daniel Lucey, Cooryleary, Bantry.

Kealkil Company
Jack O'Connor, Kealkil, Bantry.

Bantry Company
Patrick (Sonny) O'Sullivan, Milleney, Bantry.

Parson's Bridge Company
Patrick Keohane, Parson's Bridge, Bantry.

Caheragh Company
Denis O'Driscoll, Caheragh.
Willie Norris, Caheragh.

Sixth Battalion;

Adrigole Company
Michael Og O'Sullivan, Inchintaglan, Adrigole.
Matt O'Sullivan, Lackavane, Adrigole.

Castletown Company
John McCarthy (Whistler), Castletownbere.

Rossmacowan Company
Dick Spencer, Rossmacowan (wounded).

Ardgroom Company
Tim O'Shea, Droumard, Ardgroom.
John Sheehan, Barrakilla, Ardgroom. (wounded).

Eyeries, Kilcatherine and Inches Companies
Christy O'Connell, Eyeries (Section Commander).
Sean O Driscoll, Eyeries.
Tim O'Dwyer, Eyeries, Caileroe.
Pat O'Sullivan Eyeries Bawrs.
Murt McCarthy, Inches.
Jerry McAuliffe, Croumlane.
Dan O'Sullivan Gorth.
John O'Sullivan Kilcatherine.

Seventh Battalion;

Ballydehob Company
Tim Allen, Ballydehob.

Schull Company
Tom McCarthy, Schull.

Unattached to a Company in the Third Cork Brigade area:
Jeremiah McCarthy, Deeney, Skibbereen (University College Cork Company)

Scouts at Crossbarry;
Ted Finn, Crossbarry.
J. Collins, Crossbarry.
Tadgh Twomey, Crossbarry.
Paddy Cronin, Crossbarry.
Denny Doolin, Crossbarry.
Neilus Begley, Killeens.
Bill Hartnett, Killeens.
Danny Buckley, Inagh.
Miah Buckley, Inagh.
Paddy O'Leary, Ballyhandle.
Jack Falvey, Ballymurphy.
Deny Delaney, Belrose.
Jerome O'Mahony, Belrose.
Jim Lordan, Dunkereen.
Pake McCarthy, Upton.
Battie Cronin, Clashinimud.

Survivors at the unveiling of the monument at Crossbarry in 1966.

Donal Sheehan, Cork.

WEST CORK'S HEROIC DEAD

Volunteers of the Third Cork Brigade who gave their lives for Ireland in the War of Independence.

VOL. JOHN HURLEY, Moulagow,Drinagh;
1916 at G.P.O. Dublin.

LIEUT. TIM FITZGERALD, Gaggin, Bandon;
29th August 1920 at Brinny, Bandon.

LIEUT. JOHN CONNOLLY, Shannon st., Bandon;
1st October 1920 at Bandon.

VICE-COMMDT. MICHAEL MC CARTHY, East Green, Dunmanway;
28th November 1920 at Kilmichael.

LIEUT. JAMES SULLIVAN, Knockawaddra, Rossmore;
28th November 1920 at Kilmichael

LIEUT. PATRICK DEASY, Kilmacsimon Quay, Bandon;
28th November 1920 at Kilmichael

SEC-COMM. JOSEPH BEGLEY, Castle Road, Bandon;
3rd December 1920 at Bandon.

CAPT. JOHN GALVIN, South Main St., Bandon;
3rd December 1920 at Bandon.

LIEUT. JIM O'DONOGHUE, Shannon St., Bandon;
3rd December 1920 at Bandon.

LIEUT. MICHAEL McLEAN, Lowertown, Schull;
8th December 1920 at Gaggin, Bandon.

VOL. TIM CROWLEY, Behigullane, Dunmanway;
14th December 1920 at Dunmanway.

CAPT. JEREMIAH O'MAHONY, Paddock, Enniskeane;
December 1920 at Paddock, Enniskeane.

VOL. PATRICK DONOVAN, Cullnigh, Timoleague;
17th January 1921 at Timoleague.

VOL. DENIS HEGARTY, Clashfluck, Timoleague;
21st January 1921 at Courtmacsherry.

VOL. DANIEL O'REILLY, Granassig, Kilbrittain;
24th January 1921 at Bandon.

LIEUT. PATRICK CROWLEY, Kilbrittain;
4th February 1921 at Maryboro', Timoleague.

SEC-COMM. PAT O'DRISCOLL, Mohona,Skibbereen;
7th February 1921 at Mohona, Skibbereen.

VOL. PATRICK COFFEY, Breaghna, Enniskeane;
14th February 1921 at Kilrush, Enniskeane.

VOL. JAMES COFFEY, Breaghna, Enniskeane;
14th February 1921 at Killrush, Enniskeane.

LIEUT. JOHN WHELAN, Liverpool;
15th February 1921 at Upton.

SEC-COMM. BATT FALVEY, Ballymurphy, Upton;
15th February 1921 at Upton.

LIEUT PATRICK O'SULLIVAN, Raheen, Upton;
15th February 1921 at Upton.

VOL. JOHN Mc GRATH, Rathclarin, Kilbrittain;
16th February 1921 at Crois na Leanbh.

VOL. JEREMIAH O'NEILL, Knockpogue, Kilbrittain;
16th February 1921 at Crois na Leanbh.

VOL. TIM CONNOLLY, Fearnagark, Kilbrittain;
16th February 1921 at Crois na Leanbh.

VOL. CON Mc CARTHY. Kilanetig, Ballinadee;
16th February 1921 at Crois na Leanbh.

COMMDT. CHARLIE HURLEY, Baurleigh, Kilbrittain;
19th March 1921 at Ballymurphy.

VOL. JEREMIAH O'LEARY, Corrin, Leap;
19th March 1921 at Crossbarry.

VOL. PETER MONAHAN, Bandon;
19th March 1921 at Crossbarry.

VOL. CORNELIUS DALY, Carrig, Ballinscarthy;
19th March 1921 at Crossbarry.

VOL. TIM WHOOLEY, Carrycrowley, Ballineen;
22 March 1921 at Shannonvale.

CAPT. FRANK HURLEY, Laragh, Bandon;
9th May 1921 at Bandon.

VOL. GEOFFREY CANTY, Scrahan, Newcestown;
9th May 1921 at Murragh.

LIEUT. CORNELIUS MURPHY, Clashfluck, Timoleague;
11th May 1921 at Cloundreen, Kilbrittain.

VOL. DANIEL CROWLEY, Behigullane, Dunmanway;
7th June 1921 at Behigullane.

VOL. MATTHEW DONOVAN, Quarries Cross, Bandon;
10th June 1921 at Quarries Cross, Bandon.

VOL. JOHN MURPHY, Cloghane, Bandon;
22nd June 1921 at Cloghane, Bandon.

The Examiner

Tom Barry speaking at the annual Commemoration at Crossbarry (L to R): Den Doolan, Flor Begley, Tom Barry, Liam Deasy, Tom Kelleher and Mick Deasy.

THE PIPER OF CROSSBARRY.

The Piper of Crossbarry, boys, he rose ere the morning's tide,
He walked up to his Captain bold, with his warpipes laid aside,
Says he, "I've done with piping, for I'll fight for liberty,
And today, please God, we'll hold the sod and set old Ireland free."

Said the Captain to the piper, boys, upon that fateful day,
"Today you'll stride between our lines and martial music play,
For when we hear the Irish pipes, we shall strive for victory,
And today, maybe, at Crossbarry, we shall set old Ireland free."

Says the piper to the Captain, boys, "While breath is in my breast
I will chant a song of Ireland's wrong till the sun sets in the west."
And the tune he played that day of fate shall never wholly flee
For the Piper of Crossbarry, boys, he piped old Ireland free.

From Cork, Kinsale and Bandon town, from Ballincollig too,
The British poured a thousand men upon Tom Barry's few,
But when the sun had set upon that day of victory,
The Piper of Crossbarry, boys, he piped old Ireland free.

From the break of dawn the day wore on, as Crossbarry's battle rolled,
For Irish guns and Irish sons had challenged England's hold,
And when the blazing lorries flamed to signal victory,
O, the men of old Crossbarry, boys, had set old Ireland free.

So here's to brave Tom Barry, boys, and to his hundred men,
To the Lordans, Hales and Crowley, Kearney and Kelleher,
O'Connell, Deasy, Murphy, who smashed the Saxon tide,
And the Piper of Crossbarry, boys, we'll speak of him with pride.

A health to brave Flor Begley, boys, who raised the chant of war,
Who strode among the fighting men while his warpipes droned afar,
For the music of his warlike songs, it cowed the enemy,
'Twas the Piper of Crossbarry, boys, who piped old Ireland free.

Forget not those brave Volunteers who fell on that bloody plain,
For them the piper raised a dirge to caoin above the slain,
And the Banshee's sad lament was heard in the time of victory,
As the Piper of Crossbarry, boys, was piping Ireland free.

While grass is green on Ireland's scene, while the heath grows on the moor,
So long we'll talk of those who fought that Ireland might endure,
We will speak with pride of Barry's men who bled for liberty,
And the Piper of Crossbarry, boys, who piped old Ireland free.

Members of the Volunteer Brigade Pipe Band and friends
in the Summer of 1919 at Ballinascarthy Feis.
Back Row (L to R): Joe Begley, Eily O'Regan, Mick Herlihy, Tim Downing,
Pat Crowley, — , Pat Nyhan, Dolly Crowley and Jim O'Donoghue.
Front Row (L to R): Sean Daly (Pipe-Major and Instructor), Jack
Downing, Robert Begley, —, Dermot Crowley, Richie Twomey, Flor
Begley.
This is the only known photograph of Flor Begley with his warpipes.

BIBLIOGRAPHY

Printed Sources

Barry, Tom: *Guerilla Days in Ireland* (Dublin, 1949).

Birkenhead, Earl of: *Birkenhead* (London, 1935).

Brennan-Whitmore, W.J.: *With the Irish in Frongoch* (Dublin 1917).

Crozier, General F.P.: *Impressions and Recollections* (London, 1930).

Deasy, Liam: *Towards Ireland Free* (Cork, 1973).

Devoy, John: *Recollections of an Irish Rebel* (New York, 1929).

Jones, Thomas: *Whitehall Diaries (London, 1971).*

Kenneally, John: *Recollections of the Irish Revolutionary Brotherhood* (New York 1908).

MacArdle, Dorothy: *The Irish Republic* (Dublin 1951).

Macready, Sir Nevil: *Annals of an Active Life* (London, 1924).

Mitchell, John: *The History of Ireland* (Glasgow, 1862).

Ó Broin, Liam: *The Chief Secretary* (London, 1969).

O'Donoghue, Florrie: *No Other Law* (Dublin, 1954).

O'Donoghue, Florrie: *Tomás Mac Curtain* (Tralee, 1958).

O'Malley, Ernie: *On Another Man's Wounds* (Dublin, 1954).

Various Articles: *Capuchin Annuals* (Dublin, 1940-1970).

Various Articles: *The Kerryman – Christmas Number, 1937, 1938 and St. Patricks Day Number 1939.* (Tralee, 1937, 1938, 1939).

Manuscript Sources

1. Copies of personal statements prepared for the Bureau of Military History by individual members of the Third Cork Brigade.
2. Copies of personal statement prepared for the Bureau of Military History by Denis Lordan, Cork City.
3. Copies of personal statement prepared for the Bureau of Military History by Peter Kearney, Dublin.
4. Copies of personal statement prepared for the Bureau of Military History by Flor Begley, Bandon.
5. Copies of personal statement prepared for the Bureau of Military History by Frank Neville, Upton.
6. Records of the following Companies of the Third Cork Brigade: Kilbrittain, Kinsale, Timoleague, Clogagh, Kilpatrick, Bandon, Ballinadee, Ballinspittle, Barryroe, Innishannon, Crosspound, Newcestown, Farnivane and Quarry's Cross.

7. Records of Upton and Crossbarry Ambushes by Commandant Flor Begley, Bandon.
8. Records of the formation of communications system and general activities by Commandant Flor Begley, Bandon.
9. Statement of Batt Foley concerning the withdrawal of the the Flying Column from Crossbarry.
10. Letters concerning his capture and escape, and an account of the arms dumps at Raheen by Captain Frank Neville.
11. Regimental Records of the Second Battallion Hampshire Regiment.
12. Regimental Records of the First Battallion Essex Regiment.
13. Letters of Liam Deasy, Flor Begley, Sean McCarthy, Tom Barry, Paddy O'Brien, Florrie O'Donoghue, Charlie Hurley and Denis Lordan.
14. Records of the planned ambush at Shippool and the events leading up to Crossbarry ambush and his statement of the battle by Liam Deasy.